JUST IN CASE IT ISN'T THERE

POSTCARDS FROM ELSEWHERE

Volume One 1988-2001

R. NEMO HILL

DOS MADRES

2022

DOS MADRES PRESS INC.
P.O. Box 294, Loveland, Ohio 45140
www.dosmadres.com   editor@dosmadres.com

Dos Madres is dedicated to the belief that the small press is essential to the vitality of contemporary literature as a carrier of the new voice, as well as the older, sometimes forgotten voices of the past. And in an ever more virtual world, to the creation of fine books pleasing to the eye and hand.

Dos Madres is named in honor of Vera Murphy and Libbie Hughes, the "Dos Madres" whose contributions have made this press possible.

Dos Madres Press, Inc. is an Ohio Not For Profit Corporation and a 501 (c) (3) qualified public charity. Contributions are tax deductible.

Executive Editor: Robert J. Murphy

Illustration & Book Design: Elizabeth H. Murphy
www.illusionstudios.net
Cover photos: R. Nemo Hill

Typeset in Adobe Garamond Pro, Felix Titling, Iowan Old Style & Renaiss
ISBN 978-1-953252-47-0
Library of Congress Control Number: 2022931028

First Edition

But at last 'neath a yellow lotos moon,
  By the ribb'd and shelving shore,
I should bury my treasures all too soon,
  I should dream, but set sail no more.

Samuel Loveman

You can't jump a jet plane
Like you can a freight train.

Gordon Lightfoot

for
Bill Paradise
&
I. Wayan Subawa

CONTENTS

1992
ALL THINGS VIEWED THOUGH THEIR FLIGHT

1993
WHY THIS TALK OF DROWNING?

1994
THOSE WHO GO AND RETURN
(for Jay Funk)

1995

THE SIMPLEST OF DEW-HARVESTING RECIPES

1996

IN THE SUBLUNARIUM

1997
THROUGH THE LOOSENED WEAVE

1998
THE WHOLE HARVEST

1999
IT'S ALL GOING

2000
WITHIN RANGE OF THE USUAL SUFFERING

2001
IT'S SO QUIET YOU CAN HEAR THE ANTS TALKING

JUST IN CASE IT ISN'T THERE

POSTCARDS FROM ELSEWHERE

AUTHOR'S NOTE

Why *postcards*? Well, even before I acquired the blank book into which many of the details of these short pieces were recorded, I was sketching them out in numerous postcards to friends and acquaintances back home. And thus, I owe a great debt of gratitude to my many correspondents for providing me, initially, with concrete destinations for these reflections on my travel experiences. As the years passed, and my trips to Bali continued, there emerged this project of creating a collection of these musings, and yet many of them were still begun as snail-mail postcards, subsequently transcribed and modified into my daily journal, and then expanded or contracted at home in New York City where I used their scribbled details as a memory tool to recreate and preserve moments otherwise ephemeral.

I have never been able to keep a journal at home—it is only travel that has elicited any discipline in this regard. Older now, I find it a curious fact that such large blocks of my time at home in the States have slipped away, their details lost, whereas these days spent abroad remain fresh and clear thanks to my having polished these postcards, like gems, over and over again, for many years. In a profound way then, they are postcards to myself.

I also did not take many photographs for at least the first decade of my travels. I would bring one of those disposable Kodak contraptions, and a few of the photos would survive the vagaries of light and time—. But on the whole, the only technique I had of preserving impressions was verbal. This volume begins in the pre-email, pre-digital era, an era of primitive fax machines and over-priced and unreliable long-distance connections. For the first few years, even electricity was a luxury only be found in town, an hour's walk from home. It may well have been my sense of isolation then that set me to work so diligently, sending forth these postcards that took at least two weeks to get where they were going, if they got there at all. My pen became my camera, and no event seemed too minor for a quick longhand snapshot.

In composing and arranging this volume I did not intend to unfold the whole narrative of my journeys. I am present, undoubtedly, but I found myself eliminating much personal data, and much connective tissue. Rather, my intention has been to isolate certain details, impressing them on time the way they have been impressed on my mind. Travel has a way of clearing the mind, wiping its slate clean of old habits and ways of seeing, readying it for a welter of new images. I was intent on capturing those images, but gently, so as not to damage their wings. And these journals have provided me with source material for many poems as well. Indeed, readers may find here and there in this book, prose versions of formal poems that have been published in other places. I have long been a believer that poetry can be found in prose as well as in verse—as well as out in the astoundingly wide world. I have merely tried to reach out and catch it, and hold it, however I can, for that moment which lasts forever on the page.

This volume takes me up to a point where I stopped travelling for a few years, due to complications including ill-health on the heels of an HIV positive diagnosis. When my strength returned, my travels resumed, along with my journal, and I have been transcribing those years of notes as well, into a second volume, one that differs a bit from this first volume in that I am trying to be more narratively thorough. Perhaps it is my advancing age that will give *Volume Two* more of the flavor of a travel memoir, but in the meantime, I offer this flock of images.

And, with the help of memory as well as my old address books, I would like to formally express my gratitude here to my many correspondents over the years, both friends and acquaintances, including...

Samara Davis, Don Iocca, Lissie Fritz, Ariel Bloom, Michelle Slater, S Again, Tom Chomont, Michael Anthony Davis, Jay Funk, Brad Gaeddert, Rachelle Garniez, Ivan Galetti, Bill Rice, Edna & Bob Hill, Derrick Hussey, Shauna Flenady, Mark Harrington, Charlie Bergengren, Tracy Swan, Jeanne Hedstrom, Rose Kelleher, Haresh Advani, Phillip Johnston, Jude Hill, Simon Jutras, Jimmie Jobe, Joseph O'Dea, Bryn Kelsey, Charles Allcroft, Al Joseph, Mark Verabioff, Jee Leong Koh, Julio Mendez Perea, Brian Zabcik, Dan Kelly, Mark Knego, Kasmore Rhedrick, Martin Klug, Jeff Hill, Lei Chou, Michelle LaRue, Lois Collette, Bonnie and Walter, Frank Zwirlein, Douglas Landau, Lavinia Co-op, Bob Heman, Linda & Alan, Black-Eyed Susan, Brad Gaeddart, Daniel Kubert, Alan Salsbury, Michael London, Robert Vasquez, Jim Mairs, Gerri Bresler, Benjamin Marcus, Jeff DiGangi, Michael Curtis, David Winterburn, Joe Mejia, Jan Mohlman, Jim Neu, Marvin Cohen, Noufissa Bernikhou, Mary Meriam, Wallace Sanders, Rui Duarte, Austin MacRae, Rick Mullin, Willie & Alex Baer, Kevin O'Connor, Jane Ormerod, Sherri Kaplan, Peter Waring, Kursten Bracchi, Rodrigo Pascal, Alfredo Ceibul, Paco Brown, Paulo Jorge San Pinho, Shashi Musso, Raymond Childs, Alan Diggs, Orlando Ferrand, Paul Baumbach, Emery Snyder & Robert Mealy, John Marcus Powell, Richard Roberts, Rino LaDelfa, David Robinson, Rachelle Starr, Leon Sauke, Jeffrey Seeds, Michael Tatro, Joseph Smith, Thelma Lane, Clayton Smith, Robert Vasquez, Benjamin Ullon, Janis Wikoff, Phillip Zimmerman, Ulla Dydo.

R. Nemo Hill
June 2021

1988

DREAM'S MISSING CAPTAIN

The wondrous 'World of Glass' wherein inisl'd
All long'd-for-things their being did repeat;—

Samuel Taylor Coleridge

A SAILOR HAD LIVED HERE MANY YEARS AGO

22 March 1988—Andong, Bali—

A dream colleague and I are investigating haunted houses. We choose one—and after getting permission from the elderly couple who live there, we follow them downstairs. The basement is littered with huge coils of rope, sleeping like serpents amongst the anchors and figure-heads of ancient ships. A sailor had lived here many years ago—though the present residents, the aged pair, can tell us nothing about him. They are surprised by the contents of their own basement. We set to work immediately with rude invocations to the spirits, threatening and cajoling them to make their presence known—which they do, almost immediately—pounding the membrane between here and there with an infinite pulse that sets walls and floor trembling with expectation, but which stops as abruptly as it started. We are unorthodox ghost hunters, our methods grow cruder and cruder, we drop to our knees and beg, we raise our fists and curse, all to no avail—. The spirits will not return. Perhaps we are working at cross purposes? Perhaps we are frightened that our techniques will ultimately succeed? Perhaps I, the dreamer, am merely heading off a nightmare at the pass by failing at my dream profession of conjuring? These dark relics of seafaring life *are* frightening somehow. Weather-beaten and salt-stained, infested with vermin, their loneliness seems almost contagious—as if all who come in contact with them will be likewise lost, abandoned and forgotten beneath the surface of some sea. I wake up and cannot get back to sleep. I have no bottled water to drink and I'm terribly thirsty. So I reach for a candle and my notebook and begin to scribble in the half-dark like a sailor, wretched in his berth, writing in the ship's log of a vessel steered by dream's missing captain.

1991

NOTHING ELSE HUMAN
FOR AT LEAST A MILLION MILES

I see a road and a flash of lightnin'
And lemme tell ya—it's frightnin'.

John Hiatt

THE BROKEN STONE, THE RUNNING STITCH

5 March, 1991—Andong, Bali—

Rootless restless soul, or neurotic idiot—no sooner do I arrive, than I depart. Propped up on the porch with a warm wet slightly salty pillow stuck to the small of my back, I'm leafing through the pages of another place, another hemisphere, another journal kept on a trip to Portugal last year.

> *God knows I had before and have again once more*
> *now time, now reason, to walk silent, to explore*
> *with eyes cast down mile after mile—to study undeterred*
> *this wild mosaic's proudly broken surface of a world.*

Lisboa's carefully cobbled streets could never withstand the fever of weed and weather which disrupts this other world's less deliberate paths. A quick afternoon downpour—and six inches of mud suddenly sucks the sandal right off the foot, while the next morning a sudden detour of vines choked with immediate white flowers distracts the traveler from his chosen route.

> *Not to outpace the broken stone, the running stitch,*
> *the secret of all study surely lies in this.*

I sit perfectly still, reading, as the sweat hurries down the backs of my legs.

> *To walk, and walking, pass the same a thousandth time,*
> *to recognize the echo heard, and seen, within the rhyme—*
> *the secret rhythm that allows what's hidden to exist*
> *and animates all those details we might have missed.*

THE HEAT

8 March, 1991—Andong, Bali—

In a recurring fantasy I am painting pictures of figures with halos. 'It's the heat,' I suppose—classic tropical disclaimer—turning even ordinary folk into radiant hyper-ventilating saints, forging an individual nimbus, golden, glowing, for each of the ants busy hauling and hoisting likewise luminous crumbs across the furnace of my porch. It's the heat shimmer, of course—the bright trembling shadow of equatorial everything.

IN ANOTHER ROOM

9 March, 1991—Andong, Bali—

The wasp's nest just appears in only a day or two, a lump of dried mud stuck fast to the back of my door. I smash it, either exiting or entering—I forget which—and a dozen green grub-like things tumble forth. Their only available motor reflex seems this gripping instinct, for they cling with repulsive insistence to the tissue I try to clean them up with. I'm in the bowels of something forbidden, I tell myself—a trespasser exposing some secret of incubation to the light of a world it should never see.

An hour after this morning's rain three little mushrooms have sprouted up like elfin phalli from the steaming patch of roof thatch visible from my window—as I lay sometimes writing sometimes reading sometimes only sweating and breathing on the bed. The rain was preceded by another mild earthquake. The whole earth shook like a floor of old wooden planks upon which an unseen dancer beat time in another room of this haunted house which no *one* ghost will ever be able to explore entirely. Even outside in the sunshine, in the garden—locked doors will always remain.

THE RULES AND THE GAME

10 March, 1991—Andong, Bali—

All through dessert I watch the rats playing in the hollow of the restaurant's rolled up bamboo shades, running back and forth over the heads of unsuspecting diners. A brief squall of rain almost sends the staff running to unfurl the shades, almost sends the playful rats rolled up inside tumbling down onto the tables of the tourists. This morning it's ants running around the rim of a bowl filled with fruit. I recognize those frantic circles around just such a succulent center—that sweetness always just out of reach. Different games have different rules, I suppose. Sometimes it's back and forth, sometimes round and round. Sometimes it's about crossing a line, though the stakes are a bit higher in that case—like last night on my way home—. Lying across the path at my feet was a snake, one of those painfully bright green snakes I'd been warned about. I recoiled at the last moment with my foot frozen only inches from its upraised head; and confident in the strength of its venom the snake was in no hurry to move out of my way. Just what sort of noise do you make to frighten an arrogant serpent? I hissed and howled, stamped, even cursed aloud in my own language. A handful of stones hurled from a safe distance finally did the trick. Even so it was the leisurely exit of royalty that I witnessed, a slow slither into higher grass as if leaving had been the snake's own idea all along. For several moments after it vanished, a faint green glimmer lingered in its wake—a vein of emerald ore glimpsed in the depths of a dark mine, a distant memory of lightning in a forest.

SKIN DEEP IN *YOGYA*

15 March, 1991—Yogyakarta, Java—

A whole gallery of beauty salons, their little front windows crowded with portraits of men and women sporting aggressively outdated & imported hairstyles—beehives, pompadours, flips and waves and bobs, sideburns and goatees, all painted directly onto the glass. The shadows within the shops create a smooth opaque canvas for the numbed skin tones of these faces which gape and leer at passers-by. But then I catch them from behind, reflected in the mirrors lining the rear wall of each shallow shop—. Backlit now, the sun's glare pockmarks their pale cheeks and singes their jet hair with a leprous chaos of brutally illuminated brushstrokes.

Turning a corner, leaving the beauty ghetto behind, I find myself unexpectedly in the coffin quarter. Last year I saw a man sleeping through the midday heat atop one of the many coffins he'd just planed and sanded. I half expect to see him sleeping there still. I study the rows of fresh coffins. There is no sign of their exhausted, barefoot carpenter. Yet inside me he has left a single calm brushstroke, smelling of sawdust.

SERIOUS FICTION IN SINGAPORE

18 March, 1991—Singapore—

The downtown bookstores here are packed with the always up-to-date *how to,* while the age-old *what for* receives scant shelf space. A man on line ahead of me has chosen a slim treatise on public speaking—three, five, maybe ten steps to its mastery, each one no doubt quicker and more painless than the next. This man is short, presumably rather shy—and as he arrives at the state-of-the-art cash machine, over his bowed head and stooped shoulders I catch a brief glimpse of its digital caption: *SELF HELP.* The stout woman directly in front of me is clutching not one, but two books concerned with carbohydrates—pro and con views perhaps. I wince as the word *DIET* appears twice in quick succession alongside dollar and decimal on the cashier's screen of commentary, then step forward with some trepidation to have my own data-based fortune told—*$7.99 SERIOUS.*

TWO LANDSCAPES

21 March, 1991—Andong, Bali—

This morning, white cat, blue building, red skirt, all arranged on the green steps of the *sawah*—three remaining pieces on a ragged chessboard where the same match has been continuing for centuries. A plume of pale smoke rises into the sky, recalling a time even more distant than the time of the game.

Another postcard, the terraces golden now, in full harvest. On the horizon, a volcano blue as the shadow on milk. Tiny and frail in the center is a scarecrow—one long arched bamboo pole, one long frayed string, one faded red shirt, dangling. Nothing else human for at least a million miles.

ACROSS THE RIVER

4 April, 1991—Andong, Bali—

It's an intensely private Easter Sunday. All that arises, arises deep within me to the rhythm of the rice harvest across the river— *thhhwhht, whhht, thwhhht, thhhht, whht, thhwhhhht.* Through a clearing in the palms, no more than a glimpse of bent backs and broad straw hats like overturned baskets bobbing up and down on waves of heat. This side of the river is wet and green. The other side is dry and golden, scarred by the swift flash of a long curved blade descending. Incarnation is a casual affair here, here the spirit is made flesh and then dies again and again to the music of those women I can't quite see on the far bank of the river who beat the earth with their golden scythes and sheaves over and over and over again, freeing the chaff, the seed, the stone rolled away from the tomb, the soul borne away by this wind which carries the echo of their labor across the golden paddy, across the river, not to my eye, but to my ear—*thhhwhht, whhht, thwhhht, thhhht, whht, thhwhhht, thhhwhht, whhht, thwhhht, thhhht, whht, thhwhhht, thhhwhht, whhht, thwhhht, thhhht, whht, thhwhhht, thhwhhht, whhht, thwhhht, thhhht, whht, thhwhhht, thhwhhht, whht.*

BLACK AFTERNOON

5 April, 1991—Andong, Bali—

On a black afternoon storm clouds roll in veiling all color in the landscape, the white cat walking along the garden wall turns gray, the birds do their whirling prophecy number—but the apocalypse just won't materialize. Only the old man with wire limbs who's been squatting in the *sawah* cutting grass every morning since I arrived remains unaffected, continuing on with his work, not even looking up at the gathering gloom that creeps up and contains him. I can see it now—. When the apocalypse does finally arrive with or without its legendary clap of thunder, this imperturbable old man will make one gesture, only one. Still crouching, he will cough, and then simply lay his sickle aside.

ALL THE EMOTIONS

6 April, 1991—Andong, Bali—

Last night in a dream I refuse to muzzle a dog. We are performers, this dog and I, in a somewhat disreputable circus. I'd already spent much of the night tossing and turning, tortured by thought—and having finally drifted off to sleep, I find myself with this dog's snout grasped reluctantly in one hand, and with a leather muzzle dangling from the other. There is impatient calliope music, an odor of animal feces in sawdust, and a crowd of equestrian clowns and trapeze queens and human cannonballs just outside the spotlight—gesturing imperatively from the shadows, angry that I might spoil what is apparently their grand finale. From meek to rabid, the dog's expression seems to run the gamut of emotions and instincts with each tick of the dream clock—as I hold on, uncertain what to do next, yet at the same time convinced of the possibility that this state of paralysis is the most necessary part of the act.

INFINITY

20 April, 1991—Kuta, Bali—

A chubby little girl in a little bright yellow swimsuit lost her little bright yellow inner-tube on the beach this morning—the cheap plastic kind that fits round the waist like an inflated doughnut. Three times the wind stole it. Three times the wind rolled it like a wheel along the shoreline. And three times she chased it and chased it and chased it, occasionally diving in desperation and falling face-first in the sand. She'd catch it at last. She'd drag it back. Moments later the wind would steal it away again, and again she'd set out in resolute pursuit. The third time she ran so fast, so far, that I almost lost sight of her—and couldn't stop laughing and laughing and laughing at her motorized little inch long legs on the treadmill of infinite distance.

SERIOUS SEA SONG

27 April, 1991—Kuta, Bali—

Caught in a wild rainstorm on the beach around noon, I seek shelter under the nearest tree—a twisted old wreck with one or two branches and a few gnarled needles of leaves, not much of an umbrella. For over an hour I crouch there, shivering with cold, watching the rain sweep across the sand in waves more powerful than those of the surf. The old crones who hawk their wares day after day in the hot sun are crouched down all round me, huddled under bright blue plastic tarps. One even tries to sell me a coca-cola as I drip and shiver alongside her. *"Cold drink—?"* I just look at her. She scowls. Business is bad today, no doubt about it, nothing to do but sit gazing out at the driving rain and the emptied beach and the other storm-blasted trees in the distance—their black solitary scrawl scratched against a slate sky pressed against an endlessly violent white line of surf foaming. The old women flee eventually, scrambling up the dunes and across the deserted wet road, three or four at a time—bright blue tarps snapping over their heads in the wind. The rain never lets up for a moment. I sit there all alone, tarpless, and when I'm not feeling foolish or annoyed, I pretend I am a certain mad artist braving the elements in order to paint them, or a certain musician strapped to the mast of a certain ship in a typhoon, whistling serious sea songs. The walk home is an endless trudge through unexpectedly arctic tropics—cold rain running between my brows and along the bridge of my nose, pouring down my upper lip, and dripping from the tips of my uncontrollably chattering teeth.

BREAKFAST AT LINDA'S COFFEESHOP
ON LONG LAYOVER IN GUAM

28 April, 1991—Guam—

Low and flat and dark, with a corner full of pinball machines decades old and Great Balls of Fire blaring over the jukebox— its worn wooden paneling has been mellowing for years, its table-tops yellowing beneath too many coffee stains and coats of varnish. The clientele is a strange mixture, Southern Pacific American Legion, with a whiff of prostitute and hurricane—their distinctive perfumes lingering, bittersweet gardenia and sea salt, even on this dead calm weekday morning. The waitress wears a brown dress blooming with large very round very red roses. And on a stool behind the lunch counter lies a newspaper folded in half so that only the huge block letters of its headline are visible. It's upside down, and so it takes me a moment to decipher the words *SEAWEED RESPONSIBLE FOR 2nd DEATH—*. And by that time my eggs have arrived, their yellow raft of rescue afloat on what was once a white plate, with coffee in a chipped cup, a refill, the first of many for my jet-lag, plunked down within easy reach.

1992

ALL THINGS VIEWED
THROUGH THEIR FLIGHT

*As an alluring object of a prolonged gaze,
doesn't this dust of suns then commend itself
more than any star, than any constellation
to those who are lingering on one fine night over their dreams?*

Raymond Roussel

*I know that kind of man—
It's hard to hold the hand
Of anyone who is reaching for the sky just to surrender.*

Leonard Cohen

THIS ELEGANT RUSTLING OF LEAVES

9 February, 1992—Los Angeles—

The Hollywood Central Motel at Highland and Sunset doesn't seem particularly central—although nothing in Los Angeles seems particularly central. Not to mention the creeping liminality of this week of continual departures, which could push even the most persistent nucleus right up to or just beyond the edge, into this border zone. Already the list of unrecoverable details is building behind me clack clack clack clack each inch of track lost almost before the locomotive can register its passage—. The hellishly boring six hour layover in the St Louis airport. The crazy boy who followed me down dark Divisidero Street after the San Francisco bars closed and offered me meth and acid and then spit at me when I declined, all the while crooning romantic pop tunes in a tenderly homicidal whisper. The old man who had a stroke on the flight from SF to LAX. The curly haired little girl in El Coyote Mexican Restaurant who climbed all over like a chimpanzee and spilled her sticky soda on the vinyl seat cover and stood in it and sat in it twice, while her adult companion totally ignored her and went on devouring his black beans and rice. I'm waiting for a taxi now to take me to yet another airport, yet another quickstop, crapshop, bigtop, million-mile hop on outta here. Yet even in this border zone there *is* a hidden nucleus—right here, right now—at Highland and Sunset: a screen door, and the angle of the late afternoon sun which is casting screen-blurred shadows of leaves stirred by wind onto the whitewashed wall by the motel bed. At last there is no other sound but that wind in those leaves, and nothing else to look at but their ghostly quivering shadows—coaxing the restless kernel of elsewhere out from the weightless heart of nowhere. A long plane ride to go, yes, five or six more freeze-dried meals, take-off, landing, take-off, landing—but this elegant rustling of leaves will stay with me now, faithfully, for the next three months.

TORN POSTCARD

14 February, 1992—Andong, Bali—

More buildings blocking the view, more western symbols stitched onto the landscape. More *progress* and *comfort*. More fuel for the voracious ozone hole, I suppose—but who am I to buck the popular wisdom of a half century of advertising—I who have my toaster at home in New York, my hot and cold running cineplex down the street and choice of seven laundromats and pizza parlors and sex partners? Who am I to add the unspoiled Third World Postcard to my list of acquisitions?

No one here comes right out and says it, but I know they all wonder why I use so little of this brand new electricity—why I prefer a candle or two at night, or just sitting quietly in the dark watching moonlight blue the skin of my crossed legs. They're building a maternity hospital in the lot next door; they've drained the *sawah* and set up a series of temporary shacks for the workers imported along with the other raw materials from Java. On some mornings a radio shatters my favorite hour of dark peace before daylight, as the *haves* share their technological wealth with the *have-nots* by turning up the bass and the volume. This afternoon the little fat girl who lives in the shack nearest my porch is given a plastic tub to carry by her skin-and-bones grandfather. She hoists it dutifully up onto her head, and begins marching in her usual exuberant fashion—until she trips, and the tub tips, spilling a dozen knives and forks and spoons into thick, black rice field mud. Their clattering vaudeville is even louder than this morning's radio, but not nearly as deafening as my own burst of therapeutic laughter.

HEAVEN AND EARTH

18 February, 1992—Andong, Bali—

A bright red dragonfly lands on my knee while I am sitting in the hot sun reading about drawing down the influences of the stars and the planets via talismans—employing appropriate colors and shapes and sounds and the music of perfumes to lure Heaven to Earth. I look up, closing the book in my lap. A divine afternoon on the whole. Two yellow kittens, twin suns, are following a woman in a snow-white brassiere—the three of them walking quickly, in a line, on a path, on this windy day—while a child calls out in a very foreign tongue somewhere behind them. Heaven on this earth *does* pass so quickly. A moment—. Then the anchor is hauled, and the green palms waving on the horizon with the regularity of oarsmen propel the whole passionate boat of earth away into a sea of sky so vast no incantation can reach there.

I LOVE HOW WHEN IT RAINS
COWS JUST STAND THERE

22 February, 1992—Jalan Tegallalang, Bali—

Whizzing through the landscape today on the motorbike, racing the dark clouds of an approaching storm, I see several seconds of an outdoor ping pong game flash by and then vanish back into the tangle of jungle and rumble of thunder threatening. I love how when it rains really hard cows just stand there and continue eating in it. Chickens too—though they seem far less content, they let out little groans every once in a while, and their feathers look heavy and greasy. Here comes a farmer, shirtless, wading through puddles with a piece of cardboard on his head. Sometimes I wish I was just a patch of moss in a cool damp place. Sometimes I wish I was just a patch of moss on a rock in some shade.

THESE SWIFT HUMMINGBIRDS

25 February, 1992—Andong, Bali—

I walk around with one of those dried mud wasp nests stuck fast to the sleeve of my shirt for several hours—before someone points it out to me. That's why I shake my shoes out now, on those rare occasions when I put them on anymore. Nature colonizes even more swiftly than capitalism, the one gaining the other regaining ground relentlessly. My house, for example, although constructed not that long ago, is already is being transmuted into a hummingbird's nest. High atop an adjacent mango tree the tireless birds are fashioning their own home, flying over to steal a single straw at a time from my roof thatch—re-stitching the fabric of this local patch of world, re-weaving the present moment right out from under or over me. And what industrious little needles they can be, these swift hummingbirds! Infernal seamstresses, with sharp pointy beaks and bright flashing wings embroidering the air between the *here* and the *there* that you miss if you blink—.

OPEN SHUTTER

The view is the very thinnest of photographs
Probably imperceptible to go by
The thickness of the piece of glass which is
Left rough on one side, on the back; but all
This is enlarged when a more curious eye
Comes close enough for a lash briefly to touch.
                    —Raymond Roussel, The View

                    28 February, 1992—Andong, Bali—

Giordano Bruno was burned at the stake on the Campo de'Fiori, in Rome, on 17 February, 1600. Three hundred and ninety-two years later I sit in sweltering heat beneath the equator trying to harvest haiku from the triplets of image with which he filled the corners of the rooms of his castle of memory. A tree rises from the terrestrial globe and over it a sumptuous feast has been spread. In a barn fruit is smoking. In the middle of a small boat there is a writing desk which supports a throne.

It's the twenty-eighth of February, 1992. A dragon is yoked to an infinite flame. A psalter is decorated on one side with an axe, on the other with a parrot. An old woman washes the dirt from some frogs. If one sits long enough, watching the world, the world retreats to a place beyond the reach of the senses. One can chase it—but pausing for breath one realizes that in order to go there a bear skin and some dung must lie in the snow, a cat with a hook through one paw must enter a shrine, and a square of butter must be used to oil the reins. One realizes that in order to arrive there a bundle of linen carried a long way must at last be thrown onto a pyre, a smell of sulfur must pervade a forest whose trees bend in the direction of a powerful magnet, and a dust cloud must arise from a dry well at the bottom of which a man *must* be digging with a spade.

There was a tremendous storm last night. People's rooves blew off. I can't help thinking they were the lucky ones. Lying in bed, listening at 2 AM, I was enchanted by the roar of a wall of wind approaching from the west, sweeping forward ominously until it hit with a jolt so powerful it shook the foundations of my house and taught the legs of my bed to dance. In the morning the sun was bright, shining as if nothing out of the ordinary had happened. The neighbors (the lucky ones) were gathering pieces of their shattered rooves from the high grass flattened by the storm—as a burnished green beetle landed on my book, my knee, the open shutter of my window.

A wagon stops under a full moon as the driver sips from a flask. The wind trapped in a bottle makes a tumult if one listens closely. Some pieces of glass have been disguised as coins by the application of gold leaf. A sponge is used to wipe up the honey dripping from a triangle. A turtle crawls through a wheatfield with an apple on its back. A violet is cut with a sickle and then split with a chisel. On a stationary potter's wheel sits a pyramid stuck with a fork. An oracle is struck by a brick in his garden. A reed bends in a wind and an entire castle melts like molten metal. Raymond Roussel speaks from the cabin of the ship he never left as he traveled round the globe—. "I look deep into the ball of glass," he sighs, "and its transparent back becomes clear, my hand trembles and makes it, however I try to steady it, unstable."

The original triplets of image from Giordano Bruno's atrium and their locations are as follows: banquet/tree/globe (I-west corner); smoke/stable/fruit (I-south side); throne/desk/skiff (I-north side); dragon/inferno/yoke (II-north corner); axe/parrot/psalter (III-east side); old woman/dirt/frogs (III-west side); bearskin/dung/snow (III-north side); shrine/hook/cat (IV-west side); square/butter/reins (V-north corner); burden/linen/pyre (VII-north corner); magnet/forest/sulfur (VIII-west corner); dust/well/spade (VIII-west side); wagon/moon/flask (VIII-south side); wind/tumult/bottle (VIII-north side); gold leaf/glass/coins (XI-south corner); sponge/triangle/

honey (XV-north corner); turtle/apple/wheatfield (XV-west side); violet/ chisel/sickle ((XVII-south side); fork/pyramid/potter's wheel (XIX-north corner); garden/oracle/brick (XXI-east corner) reed/castle/molten metal (XXIV-south side).

— Giordano Bruno, On The Composition of Images, Signs, and Ideas, trans. Charles Doria, ed. & annotated Dick Higgins

POOR DEFENSELESS EAR

5 March, 1992—Andong, Bali—

Today is *Hari Nyepi,* another Balinese New Year. It's a day of silence—no traffic allowed on the roads, no electricity, no hustle or bustle or babble. At this particular moment, minus man and his attendant racket, I can hear the eight chickens in the yard next door as well as an occasional crowing in the distance. I can hear a million cicadas all blending into one cicada, and a million birds all remaining distinctly a million birds—especially that one hooting like an owl trapped under warm water. I can hear the wind under every trembling leaf and dogs barking and water running downhill and the buzzing of wasps circling too near my poor defenseless ear. It's an interesting concept this silence. It seems to recede the closer you get to it.

10 POINTS

B sits at his bamboo table smoking cigarettes in the heat, dreaming up currencies and correspondencies for his *Karma Board Game.* Just this morning he rescued a black and white butterfly trying to pass through the glass of a closed window, cupping it in his hands and guiding it to open air. Even these small gestures, he explained, earn one credits in the game. Without lifting a pen or a pencil, without moving a muscle except those in his smoking arm, he sits designing a series of playing cards, calculating their point value. Buying medicine for a poor epileptic boy, 20 points. Sparing a mosquito, 1 or maybe 2 points. Not demanding a refund, 5 points. Inviting a wallflower to dance, 12 points. Not littering, 3 points. Offering the last bite to someone else, 7 and a half points. Theological rumor has it that the karmic equation may be a bit more complex, a bit more elliptical than this revenge of the anecdotes implies. But—it's more highbrow than poker, more fun than the confessional, and in the end it's a pretty safe bet that the beast one meets in the labyrinth is oneself. Not flinching at the face in the mirror, 10 points, match, game.

CURRENT EVENT

9 March, 1992—Andong, Bali—

There's television now. A bit of a shock hearing its unmistakable drone seeping under bamboo shades, creeping through fern and frangipani as one shuffles up the garden path in fierce midday heat. Tomorrow night on the news I will see, before I flee home to books and candles, a boy lying dead in the street in Jakarta—after falling from a roof, electrocuted trying to free a kite tangled in some lines of power.

OUR INNER INSECT LIFE

10 March, 1992—Andong, Bali—

Last night a caravan of ants stretched all the way from the bottom of the stairs to the top, then up the wall across a ceiling beam over the doorway and on up into the southeast corner of the roof— millions of ants, tiny frantic ones along with an occasional larger member of royalty, and thousands of oval white eggs in tow. I've gotten used to this sort of thing. The legs of my bed rest in cups of water, all my food is ziplocked tight and, as they were headed away from my living area, I decided to let them be—trusting they'd complete their exodus according some Master Ant Plan and be gone by morning. Which seems to be the case when I wake with the sun and see no sign of them, at least upstairs. Downstairs, however, is another story. Apparently, they'd tired at some point during their late-night trek up the stairs up the wall across the beam over the doorway and deep into the secret recesses of the roof—. And they are gathered now, at the bottom of the stairs, on the wall, eggs and all, into one dark motionless stain about a foot in diameter. I open the front door, letting in dawn's light and light's moving shadows. In less than a heartbeat a wave of wakefulness surges through the entire army of ants and sets them moving like a storm on an electronic weather map or a spasm on a sea of raw nerves. It's a truly terrifying vision of disintegration, a psychotic's mandala of the perpetual self in involuntary torment or delight: the miraculous nightmare of our inner insect life.

ONE TOILET AT A TIME

11 March, 1992—Andong, Bali—

We go toilet shopping this afternoon for B's new house. He's decided after three years to stop squatting and buy himself that porcelain throne model for those long leisurely sit-down shits which Western cultures and constitutions guarantee to the individual as an inalienable right. People *are* coming up in the world here—and despite the fact that it's hard to make decisions in this heat, we narrow it down to two colors, lime or lemon. B decides to sleep on it. No hurry he says, one decision at a time, one toilet at a time, thus a landscape and a nation are transformed. There are casualties, of course—cast-offs of the myth of perpetual progress—one of the first being those billions of fireflies that used to swarm at night like stars come to earth, igniting the tips of the rice grasses upon which they perched, re-stitching the structure of the zodiac every thirty seconds. They seem to have retreated before the oncoming tide of electric light, spiriting away their luminous palette to some more remote corner of the planet still dark enough to paint with bright flight. Last night, however, there was a brief reprieve. The wind blew so hard and the rain fell so violently that all electricity was swept away, the wires downed or drowned. Sitting on my porch I spied a few renegade fireflies dodging or decorating the dark storm, as I sat for hours, and the wind kept blowing, and the rain kept crashing like waves breaking over my rock—a familiar sensation, even back in Manhattan. Only there it isn't rainwater or seawater that I'm drenched with, there it's budweiserwater, ice cold—. But that's a different island, a different distant seacoast, with its own more primitive customs.

DON'T ASK ME WHY THE WATER HAS TO BE PERFECTLY CLEAR

12 March, 1992—Andong, Bali—

There's a birdcall I often hear from down by the river that runs behind my temporary home. A stone makes a sound when it drops straight down into water—a sound which opens hard and abrupt, is then joined seamlessly to the sudden hollow within a single syllable, *oiit*, which in turn closes with a surprising silence. This birdcall sounds just like that—but more urgent, as if the stones that sing its song were being dropped, one at a time, in a not always regular rhythm, from thousands of miles above a perfectly clear lake of water. Don't ask me why the water has to be perfectly clear—. Or why the depth of the water through which the stone plunges *must* be identical to the distance of air through which the stone plummets before it strikes the surface of the lake. The water and the air in this bird's voice *must* be parallels. Don't ask me why—.

Now, in the evening, both depth of water and distance of air darken and, as vision fails, the entire lake is overturned. Don't ask me how a lake can be overturned—. The fossilized birdcalls, stones once more, fall back from depth to distance, from water to air. And it's a new song, a song of frogs. And it continues all night long.

So a kind of clock is wound from dawn to dusk, from dusk to dawn—one which doesn't actually *tell* time but rather *helps* time to pass with a grace which precision only dreams of.

DARKER

15 March, 1992—Andong, Bali—

At dusk, waiting. Waiting to leave the hemisphere tomorrow morning. Waiting for a friend to pick me up for dinner in town tonight. Waiting patiently for my horoscope and my fingerprints to change. It gets dark while I am waiting, darker and darker—as it tends to do at dusk. The neighbors light a trash fire directly beneath an almost full moon whose edges are dissolving in mist, as are the edges of the fire below, as am I, and my horoscope, and my fingerprints, all of us, dissolving into darker and darker mist—as things tend to do at dusk. The two fires, the lunar and the other, seem symmetrical—two ends of a magic wand—as above, so below. Except for the fact that the moon is in solitude (it isn't dark enough yet for stars). Whereas the halo of burning trash is accompanied and occasionally crisscrossed by shadows, by the silhouettes of those people watching it, tending it, poking it, living around it. And later, returning after dinner, I find the bright little stinking terrestrial fire has gone out. Whereas the moon is still glowing right through the mist—darker, darker, darkest.

HAZE & ACHE & ITCH

18 March, 1992—Andong, Bali—

Some days I just can't concentrate. Singapore was archly pragmatic as usual. Shivering on an escalator in one of its monstrous air-conditioned malls, I fought back the impulse to defecate sloppily in public and bought a pair of pants instead. I'm not sure why, they're too long and the cuffs don't roll up gracefully. I'll never wear them. On the airplane, in one direction, I read William Blake; in the other I sat next to an old man who sucked his molars after a tasteless dinner. Today I'm back in Bali with my new visa, it's calm, it's peaceful, it's nearly silent—yet I can still hear that tongue on those teeth, I'm annoyed by every bird and tree and cloud and degree of heat, I have a rash backache headache sore foot even my brain is itchy. No cure for it but to sit staring at the volcano on the horizon which has been uncharacteristically visible all day long, shorn of its usual cloud cover, hard and blue and sharp-edged as a knife. Some days everything in the foreground is haze and ache and itch. Some days only the distance cuts and clears.

DOUBLE MOON

19 March, 1992—Andong, Bali—

I think my house was just struck by lightning. The electricity was off, but the bulb over my head crackled with light and fire—and then went dark again. So much rain today, the rice fields overflowing. I'm in a boat now, surrounded by sheets of water reflecting everything everywhere—which means two full moons tonight, one above, one floating below—which means the dogs will be at it again. Last night they woke me up, last night it was as if they'd all caught the same apocalyptic virus passing through their landscape like the lit fuse of a bomb in a cartoon. Sometimes it seemed as if every dog in the universe were barking and howling at once. And then it would subside, quickly—their sudden silence as mysteriously contagious as their clamor moments earlier. Anyway, they'll be fighting and fucking up a storm again tonight with this extra full moon reflected in the piece of wet silk that the rain has wrapped around the earth. The sky's already clearing. Palms are growing silvery. Already I hear an initial howl or two in the distance. And soon the Balinese calendar will be joining in the song—for no full moon passes without a full night of gamelan music drifting up from the temple down by the river to serenade the wakefulness of the gods, and the sleeplessness of mad dogs and men alone.

I VOW TO CEASE ALL SCRATCHING
AT EITHER END OF THE SPINE

21 March, 1992—Andong, Bali—

A strange and fitfully instructive night of sleep due to the annoying itch of this rash on my balls—. My scratching in search of relief *and* my rational efforts to solve some other more naggingly abstract problem, they are ultimately woven by dream into a single activity, a single desire for release from all forms of irritation. It's hard to remember now, harder to explain, but somehow in the dream I become aware of this juxtaposition of itchy testicles and itchy brain—and longing for rest in both body *and* mind, I vow to cease all scratching at either end of the spine. To this oath taking "I" of the dream are immediately revealed the secrets of a simple system linking poetry to various portions of the body in order to relieve it of its pesteredness. I am given one phrase as an example—a phrase of such beauty that I lay quite still, lost in it, with my hand finally freed from its incessant *scratch scratch scratch.* Keeping the phrase constant before my mind's eye, I am inspired to create analogous phrases for each portion of my tension afflicted body and thus to build—from the balls up, as it were—a new parallel body by manipulation of these poetically charged and regenerated verbal members. I am soon in a deep sleep, the itch (though still present) has ceased to annoy, and the lovely echo of that first phrase of my new body goes on haunting the peaceful depths in which I now find myself.

MY PAPER SACK FULL OF PRAYER

22 March, 1992—Andong, Bali—

I'm feeling a bit molten-headed after a long afternoon spent digging flowerbeds in the sun on an empty stomach. Tonight is the first night in weeks without torrential rain and cool winds at dusk—it's still and hot, I'm sun-burned and bone-tired. If my errand-runner doesn't return from town soon with my paper sack full of supper I'm going to be in the anxiously meta-theological position of proving or disproving the Sufi ascetic's ecstatic or hysteric pronouncement: *"Under my garment there is nothing but God!"*

It is possible that one day I will see Him *"face to face, alone to the alone"*—but tonight, call me weak, call me slave to sense—tonight I'll settle for his theophany in food. What obsessed me to brutalize myself so today? Shut up with my books and my verse, with my very private projects and exclusive woes, I took Rabindranath Tagore's wildly joyful admonitions quite literally to my clogged heart—. *"Whom dost thou worship in this lonely dark corner of a temple with doors all shut?"* he asked me. *"Open thine eyes and see thy God is not before thee!"* God's in the garden, of course—tilling the hard ground, path-breaking stones, even baking mudpies, *". . . and his garment is covered with dust."* From a tremendous distance Abu Taleb al-Makki sings out in true accord—*"For just as the seed does not grow but from dust, so the seed of wisdom does not grow but from the dust of the heart."*

I have a prayer of my own tonight. Half-starved and sun-stroked by a long day of religious discipline with trowel and hoe, my freshly paroled heart slipping out between the bars only to be beaten nearly senseless by the loave-ness of the loaves, by the fishy-ness of the fishes—I cry aloud, *"Christ Almighty, where's my dinner?"*

BLOSSOM AND DECAY

26 March, 1992—Andong, Bali—

Haven't heard from J. I'm worried about his health. So I telephone today, and leave a brief message. It's strange to hear his voice caged and cramped by the habitually mechanized context of a New York City answering machine—especially crouched down as I am in a different sort of cage, squatting in the dim hot cinderblock backroom of the restaurant of *Petulu Inn* as they are about to tear its roof off. They just can't stop building here. It seems a compulsion. The restaurant is only a few years old, it never opened to begin with, and now they're already demolishing it to build a drugstore which may never open either. All day long the boys have been busy uprooting plants from the beautiful garden they'd cultivated to temporary perfection. Inside this hot airless tomb of a room I squat, sweating in the dark, clutching at a black plastic receiver through which I'm listening to another side of the world. Outside in the glare, lush flowering plants are trundled from here to there, from one side of the garden to the other. Lean and bronze and shirtless, with perfect teeth and splayed toes, these endlessly toiling youths seem to draw as close to eternity as is humanly possible. Their garden will go on changing shape, one repetitive task at a time, there will be no rest for them, one back-breaking day linked to another without complaint, without comment almost—only '*biasa biasa*'—because it's all the same, good fortune, catastrophe, luck, loss, it's all only '*normal normal*'—because there's blossom and there's decay, blossom and decay, and because blossom and decay are the only sure way to measure each day.

MEDICAL ATTENTION

27 March, 1992—Andong, Bali—

Friday night in Denpasar there are four of us, each seeking a different doctor—mine is the skin and genital specialist as this testicular fungus is beginning to exhibit distinctly fascist tendencies. I feel like a beast in a cattle car or an underpaid extra in a silent film comedy projected at twice the recommended speed. It's a single mute woman dressed in white who is responsible for all entrances and all quick exits. She shoves me into one of many tiny cubicles, zips a curtain shut behind me, orders me to drop my pants, and disappears. Seconds later a doctor arrives, his white a little less bright than hers. He too vanishes before I can utter a word. My pants are still around my ankles when the woman returns, un-zipping the curtain so abruptly it sounds as if she's torn it in two. She begins to beckon impatiently as I do my own quick-zip and stumble out through the throng of the as-yet undiagnosed. And like a drop of mercury, there she is—quick, bright, silent, already waiting at the door, a prescription in one hand, the other hand extended for payment—according to my calculations approximately one thousand *rupiah* per second.

IN GREEN SPACE

31 March, 1992—Andong, Bali—

One plant seems to grow two feet overnight, one fallen crumb attracts ten species in ten minutes, one second of silence is quickly filled by an infinite cataract of birdsong. And every night after I blow my candle out and tuck myself securely underneath my mosquito netting, the entire room fills up with rats and lizards that eat or carry off everything I haven't tied or bolted down. This morning, first light reveals more than a million fragrant white trumpets, raw scarlet in the center where the sex is—they've just appeared in the field by my porch, blossoming instantaneously in green space. Ever since then each white flower has been shrieking "Now! Now! Now!" What a rude shock to realize how much of creation fits into a single moment, a pulsation of Blake's artery: each spurt, a world.

STONE OR STRAW

*He did what he alone could do, purified, as well as he could, his
house, and opened his doors, established a precarious order in the heart
of his chaos; and waited for his guest.*
> —James Baldwin

> *4 April, 1992—Andong, Bali—*

I remember sitting on my bed and breathing tears at one
point—years ago, in my little lonely house-of-stone in Pobral,
in Portugal. That was my first taste of self-imposed exile. Here,
this year, in my little house-of-straw, for reasons I don't fully
understand, that taste has returned, though without the tears.
And I find myself filled with nostalgia for the daily rituals of my
stone sojourn there, for those habits I'd acquired for so many
months—only to shed them immediately upon departure. When
we are alone—not just separate, but really alone—whether straw
or stone—minutiae loom large, time itself becomes visible, and
focus ritualizes even the most minimal actions. On the door
that led from the stone kitchen to the stone living room, I'd
taped a series of homemade calendars—one neatly ruled paper
checkerboard for each of the months of my indefinite stay. No
day passed unwatched, each day cancelled with a large quiet X
from the black felt-tipped pen which I kept balanced on the
ledge above the door. Twice a week I would buy bread, fresh out
of the oven, from a woman who always wore a flour-dusted blue
kerchief, and her mother who always wore a flour-dusted black
kerchief. The bread would be hot, almost too hot to tear with my
bare hands, and the butter would melt on contact and run down
my wrists. I'd always stop myself before finishing the whole
loaf, wrapping the last scrap in brown paper and placing it in
the middle of the kitchen table—next to my flashlight, and my
bundle of maps. I had a cassette tape of the *Berlioz Requiem*, and
a cheap Sony Walkman whose headphones buzzed mercilessly
under the onslaught of each brass fanfare. Festooning my
stairwell, were the long taped-together strips of my typewritten

novel-in-progress, the tale of a pre-adolescent sleepwalker. Each night I climbed that stairway of patchwork fiction up to my own bedroom where, despite near-freezing temperatures, I would fling open the one small window in the thick stone wall before climbing under the covers.

Why do I have that sensation again this year, that nostalgia for an unrecoverable present? I'm worried about J, mortality nags, but that doesn't explain it, that is merely a symptom of it. So I take refuge, once again, in *this* moment's tiny quotidian: lighting that stick of incense each afternoon, and inserting it into the little crack in the north wall; rinsing the coffee grounds from my cup each evening, and dumping them off the porch where they splatter the leaves of the hibiscus; slipping into my hooded gray sweatshirt each morning, and sitting beneath the porch thatch, sipping hot tea in the chill before dawn—a book closed on my lap—waiting for the warmth and the light of the sun rising.

ALL THINGS VIEWED THROUGH THEIR FLIGHT

10 April, 1992—Andong, Bali—

At dusk, an hour equals a century of uncertainty. Thus this evening I sit for a hundred years watching herons fly north to their nests as they do each and every night, threading the needles of sun and moon with the same fine line of flight. A floating wedge appears from behind me, it rises over the horizon of my shoulder, over the horizon that I am—and with eyes sailing forth I try to keep effortlessly gentle pace with the beating of wings. Whiter than the pale blues fading from the sky, whiter even than the deepening white of darkening clouds, at their most distant the birds begin to shimmer and lose form, trembling like steam, like heat, almost invisible yet never quite gone. As a transparent curtain stirred by wind distorts all that lies beyond it, so all things viewed through their flight return as ghostlike as the herons themselves to haunt the eye enchanted by an hour or a century of twilight.

RENTED ROOM WITH BLUE CURTAINS

16 April, 1992—Kuta, Bali—

Back on the coast, I'm stretched out once more on the bed, beneath the whirring ceiling fan, in the rented room with blue curtains that billow inward all night long like a box of sky collapsing. Returning home after months of travel is one thing— home, hearth, harbor, these things are *supposed* to endure, to reassure with their stability, with their ability to happen again and again just the way they did the first time. But returning to a place one does *not* call home has quite the opposite effect— for the landmarks of travel must remain ephemeral to save the traveler from a growing sense of his own insubstantiality. Can it be that the entire world endures, while I alone merely haunt the scenes of the lives of others? This morning in a cafe I sit watching young men unload enormous blocks of ice from a truck parked in the street—the same street, the same truck, the same young men as last year. It is only me who has melted away like this ice in this heat. I alone am the mirage that comes and goes according to the angle of the light and the price of a plane ticket.

THE BALLAD OF WAYAN DENES

23 April, 1992—Kuta, Bali—

I dream about the devil and Phyllis Diller in one night. The devil scratches me with a tooth or a thorn, and Phyllis Diller reveals her true first name: *PHINONECA* (which seems as I write it down to have a distinctly satanic ring to it). Where such satanic rituals fit into these lazy days in the sun is beyond me. I see so many more people here than I do up in the mountains, and slip through so many more situations, that my landscape is increasingly littered with stray puzzle pieces. Yet they all disappear at the water's edge—even my favorite Legian Street cripple with pretzel legs and tarnished silver teeth, even Wayan Denes who wears a size 41 shoe and works seven days a week for peanuts, even Phinoneca Diller and Beelzebub—a few hours in the sun and then a dive into the ocean and the whole irreconcilable pack of details dissolves, leaving behind only a slight sting of sea salt soon blinked away from the corners of my eyes.

WRITER'S GRASP

It's difficult to write this because my hand is ill. I've damaged my wrist somehow, doing push-ups perhaps, perhaps tumbling through surf. Or perhaps I am simply writing too much—curing block with cramp, treating one malady with the next malady and the next—evolving toward more total collapse. Last night I got drunk. I went to a beachfront disco early, before they'd cleared the tables away for dancing tourists and wannabe decadent locals. The place was almost deserted. I drank my slow cold beers and watched four vertical rows of yellow lantern light gaining length and strength as darkness fell. The chatter of a few diners teased my ear like a human windchime in the background of light and shadow. Slightly dizzy, I walked home along the beach—threatened by barking dogs and the roar of nearly invisible surf. I had no hangover this morning. Just this ache in my hand. Perhaps I was holding my beer bottle too tightly, as tightly as I grip this pen.

I SUGGEST THAT HE SING TO ME INSTEAD

25 April, 1992—Kuta, Bali—

At first, I judge him to be just another precocious fifteen-year-old hustler, another mercenary on the beach at night. I think by veering closer to shore, by actually wading into the surf, I'll discourage him. But he follows—pedaling his bicycle right into shallow water. He's a lot younger than fifteen. And he asks me to sing to him, to sing some American songs. *Saya malu malu kucing,* I tell him, *I'm shy, shy like a cat—*. I suggest that he sing to me instead—which he does, serenading me softly with bits & pieces of Indonesian pop tunes as stars peek through thinning clouds and his bicycle tires hiss, making circles in wet sand.

1993

BUT WHY THIS TALK
OF DROWNING

*Time was a vast sea that swallowed me, and my soul emerged
from its anguished, tenebrous innards covered by memories,
as if it had lived a thousand years. I would compare myself to
that knight from an old legend about Santiago de Compostela who,
having been shipwrecked, emerged from the depths of the sea
with his chain-mail covered with shells...*

Ramon Del Valle-Inclan

BUT WHY THIS TALK OF DROWNING?

20 February, 1993—Amsterdam—

On my last day in Amsterdam, Vermeer's woman in blue refuses so calmly to look at me that I stand before her for over an hour, unable to write the lines of the letter she is reading. I wonder, after she raises her eyes at last and lays her letter aside, whether she too will feel this desire to walk and go on walking—despite the chill in the air, and the still cold water of the narrow canals—too black to reflect a stormy sky? It's suicide water, I remember whispering calmly to myself, its chill will numb anyone who plunges into it, its darkness will soon swallow and hide and forget one—. But why this talk of drowning, of numbness, of invisibility? The solitude of the journey, the blue of Vermeer, the letter whose contents remain forever unknown, unwritten, unread—. At the point of embarkation all that remains unsaid can thrill one to the breaking point.

THE ARTS OF PRAYER

9 March, 1993—Petulu, Bali—

B interrupts me this afternoon with a tall tale about a tiny praying mantis. I am reading Saint John of the Cross—marveling at his beautiful step by step ascent to God—yet wary at the same time of his terrifying aspiration toward total mystical union. Sitting here peacefully in the garden, this burning desire to overcome Nature in order to attain a divine union outside its bonds seems almost blasphemous, unbalanced, disrespectful to that quietly reflective knowledge gained in and through the created world. The Saint turns so completely away that I sense an act of *hubris*, a dangerous presumption which might result in a re-christening— as if I were suddenly reading the journals not of Saint John of the Cross but of Saint Frankenstein of the Castle. It's not that I don't relate to the ascetic's passion. I too feel a frustration, as I grow older and more disillusioned, a frustration with things as they are—an inability to satisfy the yearnings of soul, a desire to leap beyond sense toward something more intoxicatingly real and perfect and poetic. Love of God? Insatiable ego? Artist's vocation? Or just another hard-on, or alcoholic relapse? Of course, there are days when I just hate everybody and everything, days when I wish it would all simply go away, but I hardly think it advisable to base a theology on such sentiments as those— though I'm sure it's been done. And then B arrives and brings me back to the present garden, far from either monastic's cell or madman's castle. "I was looking down at my hand," he says, "not thinking about anything in particular." That alone sounds lovely. "It was just a speck, a spot, I thought maybe it was an ant. But it wasn't—." It was a baby praying mantis! Resting in perfect stillness on the back of his hand! Infinitesimal! Flawless in the complexity of its form and yet almost transparent, almost invisible to the naked eye! B doesn't stay long, just long enough for a bit of playful exaggeration—chatting on about flea circuses and trained crickets and the outrageous possibilities given what he claims to be the superior intelligence and grace of a praying mantis. Minutes later he roars off on his motorcycle. And I am left here with my holy mountain of books and thoughts, doggedly climbing up and on toward mystical union with my own hopeful hand.

PARADISE

11 March, 1993—Petulu, Bali—

My expatriate friend has been designing birdhouses all week.
I've been discussing the price of eggs with a young Balinese boy.
"In one place they're twice as expensive as another," I observe.
To which he replies, in abruptly perfect English: "*The Economic
Principle.*" Over his shoulder, in the hot sun, I see yet another
gaggle of Japanese or German or American girls, in sweat-stained
shorts and halter-tops and backpacks, toiling up the hill on their
rented bicycles in a desperate flight from just that banal reality my
young Balinese friend so proudly embraces from his privileged
pedestal in the shade of what the brochures call *paradise*. It is true
that after spending so much time here I feel somewhat stripped of
illusions—. But along with flat facts and bare bones there *is* still
the indestructible postcard of purple volcano piercing the clouds
of even an average dawn; still the conquest of fruits and flowers;
still a sun hot enough to induce psychedelic ecstasy and generate
spontaneous birdhouse architecture. Not to mention the tallest
palms across the road which are so mysteriously elegant that it
is impossible to know during a violent afternoon thundershower
whether the wind is tangling or combing their green hair.

DENTAL COSMETICS

14 March, 1993—Petulu, Bali—

I'm lying in a strip of sun, baking on hot porch tiles, sucking up bright light like a thirsty diamond— though my jaw is still aching from yesterday's budget root canal. Moments before plunging her needle into my condemned nerve, the dentist, an unusually tall Javanese woman wearing far too much make-up for the tropics, testified that she wanted only to make people look and feel more beautiful. My self-image seems entirely unaltered by such earnest surgery—but I did enjoy watching the little green lizards darting about on her office walls while she worked. Any sudden movement and they'd disappear behind one the garishly framed certificates of authority tilting over her shoulder as she hunched in closer for the nerve-kill. I thought about telling her that many years ago a friend had suggested my crooked teeth looked as if someone had thrown them in my mouth. I changed my mind at the last minute, wary of belittling her craft while so many of her sharp tools lay so near at hand.

MARMALADE

23 March, 1993—Petulu, Bali—

This morning the word *marmalade* bounces through the garden, over the hedge, and up the tiled steps of my porch at least a dozen times. In the bungalow next to mine a retired British school-teacher, come to Bali for an unprecedented experience, finds his first breakfast without *marmalade* in forty or fifty years just a bit more of an adventure than he'd bargained for. Apparently, he's convinced that if he just repeats the word out loud, louder and louder, he can somehow conjure the sweet sticky stuff of comfortable routine. I eye my own cup of black coffee with suspicion.

My favorite part of each day is the dark hour before dawn, before anyone else is awake, when I can convince myself that nothing really exists at all beyond a few lingering crickets and a slight breeze. Daybreak brings back details, yes—names, dates, burnt toast, missing marmalade. And yes, I *do* enjoy the complexity of a fine piece of embroidery as much as the next fellow. Yet it is one of the indescribable delights of a quiet life to stare at a few simple nouns and forget about all the adjectives for a while.

BUTTERFLY WITH BIG RED FLOWER

29 March, 1993—Petulu, Bali—

for Thomas Fucaloro

Outside, a butterfly as big as a bird is bothering a red flower as big (so a friend once described summer roses in Portugal) as a baby's head. The sky is overcast and sticks to my skin like glue. Time has a way of dissolving, rather than passing, on a day like today—I lay down a lot and watch the elastic waistband of my underpants darken with the sweat that pours forth from the effort it takes to observe a bird-sized butterfly sucking every last drop of sweetness from a fragrant red baby's head.

I SEEM TO REMEMBER SAYING THANK-YOU AT LEAST ONCE

I contrived to live a regular life there, orderly,
without contact of any kind, among books and flowers.
                    —Valery Larbaud

6 April, 1993— Petulu, Bali—

As I write it's getting dark, and a big round melon of moon has started to grow and glow through the bamboo. Two of the local boys walk by, barefoot, on their way to shower in the garden out back—turning on the lamps along the path as they pass by in silence. They'll leave a little lozenge of pale soap behind them, nestled in wet grass or caught between slippery green stones. As the bats make their first few swoops and dives of the night, I sit here trying to recall if I've spoken aloud at all today. I seem to remember saying *thank-you* at least once—. But that was this morning, already so long ago. I read, sit in the sun, write, sweat, shower, peel fruit, shell peanuts, and shave every fifth day—all without a word. So much of what one says, says itself, when left unsaid.

BALL OF BLUE FIRE

7 April, 1993—Sanur, Bali—

I'm riding to the dentist on the back of Wayan's motorbike, speeding through a dusk that is gathering both the promise and the threat of rain into the same beginnings of a breeze. I look up and see a sun bruised and blued by cloud, cooled by the weight of the late hour. I stare right at it without blinking. Earlier, nearer to noon, I'd been reading the ancient Hermetic Hymns to this same sun—or was it the same sun? *That* sun had been blinding—Visible God of the Cosmos and World Wheel Apparent, Ouroboric Divine Furnace of the Realm of Becoming, Burning Yolk of the Universal Egg, and Great Big Ball of Fire in general!

It is chaos on the highway here, congested and lawless, a dangerous carnival ride for reckless children, stray dogs, and runaway machines. It keeps me on a sharp uncomfortable edge. But as we speed along, dodging erratic traffic, I find my eyes not on the road, but rather in the sky, in the cool blue sun above me. Beyond me is somehow suddenly within me now, as long as my eyes continue to rest — *there* — at the whole chaotic whirlpool's hot and cool blue center glowing even as it fades. I know nothing can harm me.

ASLEEP AT THE WHEEL

10 April, 1993—Denpasar, Bali—

The plot is so thick at this point that it'll stand up in itself like a spoon in cement, yet still the recipe calls for more— more suffering more unpleasant surprises more more more of anything and everything. I spend the entire day in Denpasar Hospital where B has been deposited, broken and bleeding, after his motorbike was totaled in Ubud this morning. I'd already packed my bags near dawn, and was growing restless, nothing to do, waiting to leave Petulu for the coast at Kuta. I just lay on my back on my bed from which the mosquito netting had already been removed; I just stared out a window filled with leaves of trees blanched a pale electric green by intense sunlight. A strange calm came over me. I crossed my arms on my chest. I placed my feet neatly side by side like a corpse quiet in a coffin, or a mummy in a tomb. I guess I was pretending to be dead, sort of trying it on for size. Yet all the while I was looking, looking, even while my eyes were closed—looking so intently that I'm surprised I didn't see the accident itself as it happened—. For it happened, I'm more and more convinced, precisely at that moment.

The driver of the van that veered out of control claims later to have fallen asleep at the wheel. It seems there were a lot of us playing dead this morning—but B is by far the least co-operative volunteer for the Big Sleep. Delirious with pain, and pain killers, he keeps bashing his two plaster casts tirelessly against the metal railing of the bed and crying out for someone to go fetch the amaretto-flavored cookies he's left in his kitchen cabinet back home. *Never waste a single crumb of pleasure,* I hear a voice bellowing in my head each time the metal railing crashes and rattles beneath a fresh blow from his useless hands. At one point we have a little sing-a-long, a little last resort emergency room vaudeville. He can't remember who he is or who I am but he has no trouble at all remembering the lyrics to *I'll Be Seeing You In Apple Blossom Time.* A few hours later the apple blossoms have already faded. Swept away by some breeze or other, they've been forgotten—and so he won't believe me when I tell him we'd actually been singing aloud. But I'm quite sure the wounded in that ward will never forget the shock of such a strange serenade. Had they not been incapacitated by their own injuries, moaning and groaning with their own cuts and fractures, I'm certain there would have been a thunderous ovation—*"More! More! More! More of anything and everything!"*

SILENT WOUND

11 April, 1993—Denpasar, Bali—

There's a little square of emergency room gauze balanced on the bone-deep cut on your forehead. It keeps slipping off. It keeps falling to the floor. I lose count of how many times a doctor or a nurse, hurrying by, barefoot, picks up the filthy bloodstained bandage and presses it back into place. It's like that scene in an old black & white silent film where a hand is placed over the mouth of a woman about to scream—but the mouth, the wound, the slit in the head is, in this case, bright red.

STILL RUNNING

14 April, 1993—Kuta, Bali—

I have new neighbors in my garden—two black and white dogs, mother and pup, who run madly about all day, day after day, chasing one another through the bushes like electrons whirling around no nucleus. Meanwhile B lies somewhere in a Singapore hospital having his wrists reassembled under a fluoroscope, and keeping that stiff upper lip—which is always a sure sign of the jello just beneath the surface. Packing my bags a few hours ago I peeked out the window, through stiff black shutters and soft slow blue curtains billowing inward—and there they were, still running round and round, rustling through the huge dry fronds fallen from the row of banana palms that rim the high stone wall.

I'm sitting in the airport now, far from the garden, on my scalloped orange plastic chair. I can't see them—but I know they're still running—. Just like I know the surf is still rolling even though the last windowful of it vanished hours ago when the car I was riding in turned inland, shifted gears, and sped off down the highway. Just like I know that at dusk tomorrow evening and every evening after that, along every road on the entire island, figures will emerge and gather in front of their homes, perched on stoops of stone or stumps of wood or just squatting on their haunches—talking, laughing, flirting, arguing, or just watching traffic pass or twilight shadows fall or dogs, black and white dogs perhaps, chasing one another—across the road over the wall through doorway and ditch and out into the garden beyond, running through dusk toward night until all disappears in darkness. Latest call for my repeatedly delayed flight is ten o'clock—that's twenty minutes from now, twenty more minutes running on and on ticket taken like electrons seat-belt fastened whirling round no known nucleus.

MAGIC BOX

23 April, 1993—Rijks Museum, Amsterdam—

(Philipp Hainhofer,
for Hertog August van Bronswijk-Luneburg
Augsburg ca. 1630)

In the topmost panel Saint George and the Dragon are fading away,
fading away. The face of the saint is primitive, almost egg-like in a
way that blurs the line between religious ecstasy and mental handicap.
His wings are blue and his robe is red—but once again the whole
tableaux is so faded that it seems as if viewed through an amber haze
of infinite depth. In his left hand the saint holds a long staff. In his
right, maybe, a golden feather. The dragon is a yellow crocodile.

The inner surfaces of the two open side doors are slices of patterned
marble, reddish brown in color. In the lower sections the marble
has been worked into the design to suggest a foundation of rocks, a
promised stability, a ground. To the right, a man with blue wings
and a red tunic over a white shirt. In his right hand a staff which
strikes the ground, and under his left arm a large blue fish out
of water. He's walking towards the center. On the other side, also
walking towards the center, is another blue-winged man in a light
green tunic and a pale red skirt. In his right hand another grounded
staff. In his left a golden cup or grail, raised to the sky. Beyond both
winged men, on the distant horizon, are bits of a blue city emerging
from the veins of the marble. And there are winged cherubs, flying
heads without bodies, in all four corners.

The central panel is ruled by a circular echo which ripples inward
from a gilt border toward a ring of clouds from out of which more
cherubs emerge—three above, one below, one on the left with a staff,
and two on the right with a blue globe banded with gold between
them. Deeper in, the clouds are transmuted to fabric flowing into
the echo of the next circle, a blue circle, the circle of the Virgin's
dress and the crescent directly below her feet. Above, there is another

reverberating red circle for her torso, then a head placed atop that, and finally a highest halo of bluest stars. But all these circles are penetrated boldly by the Christ Child who stands in her lap— appearing in all spheres simultaneously.

In another circle, in another center, is an image that seems to glow in comparison with all the somber browns which surround it. It is Christ at the Last Supper, but alone, with no other guests. The table is a white cloth draped over his knee, littered with golden implements of mysteriously impractical design. His sleeves are red, his loose- fitting vest is blue, and he seems framed in a doorway of some sort. Around him are various reliefs—all quiet brown landscapes and a few empty abstract spaces heavily trimmed in ivory. The only other color is on the doors of the two inmost panels—where there are hints of the deep greens of distant natural scenes. These panels seem almost tapestry-like, as if one could see the individual threads with which they are not really woven.

Whole classrooms full of children come and go, as the eyes of various museum guards skim the back of my neck and the pages of my notebook like rodents sniffing suspicious trash. Maybe I shouldn't have taken my shoes off—but after two barefoot equatorial months, and then hours and hours pacing the canals in heavy steel-toed boots, my blisters overcome my museum etiquette. What a relief it is, later, to find Vermeer's woman still reading her letter, radiant as memory would have her. This time I am especially captivated by the map fastened to the wall behind her head, the skin tones of her face blending so gracefully with its distant indiscernible continents.

So, she remains. So, I depart. How foolish to think I could ever reconstruct this Magic Box from my jumbled labyrinth of notes—my marble doors and distant green scenes and pale pathetic saints with blue wings and red sleeves and a heavy ivory trim of adjectives. Up from the amber haze I must now rise. Dusted, encrusted with the music of lost spheres, I emerge from a sea which fades away immediately, sinking back into the sand like the water of a receding wave and spiriting away all the weightless days and hours and minutes and other ornaments of an always escaping magic.

1994

THOSE WHO GO AND RETURN

for Jay Funk, 1959-1994

I have turned the wheel of the horror of those who go and return.
In many places all that remains of me is a circle of gold
in a handful of dust.

O. V. de L. Milosz

THE DEATHBED WILL BE

6 June, 1994—Kuta, Bali—

How can it be? The panic of departure every time—and every time the peace of arrival. How many times must one pass through that uncountry of tense uncertainty before one learns that the other place *does* actually exist? I suppose the deathbed will be no exception to the anxious rule. No need to pretend with mock-heroic calm that I will not be seized with panic moments before the next continent rises on the horizon with perfect naturalness. Is it really necessary—this neurotic contest between gain and loss, between what lies far ahead and what falls far behind? And yet it would be but false solace merely to trust, blindly, in the infinitude of the future, the unknown—when the real problem stems from the whole linear map one constructs to begin with. Why place oneself in between at all? What exactly *are* the cartological alternatives?

Too many questions. In the meantime, I've arrived—returned! And it is all still here, still tuned to the music of the mechanical flaws in the ceiling fan rotating rotating rotating overhead. It's two hours before dawn—dark, quiet—the only really quiet part of the day here in crowded Kuta. Leaning into a desperately hot shower, I picture drunken carousing tourists and wretched barking dogs—*both* stilled at last, *both* lying, side by side, sound asleep in the same bed. My coffee is already brewing. My stinking transcontinental graveclothes are already wadded up in a ball and stuffed into the bottom of my otherwise empty laundry bag. I drop down onto the edge of the bed, heavy as an anchor, studiously avoiding my reflection in the bedside mirror—just in case it isn't there.

CORNUCOPIA

7 June, 1994—Kuta, Bali—

It's always right in the middle of the play that our unwitting traveler enters—never at the beginning. And oh, how quickly the ice-bearing boys re-freeze into perfect presence. This morning in front of *Made's Warung* as their truck pulls away from the curb, dripping water, leaking cold steam and boyish laughter— another delivery truck immediately takes its place, a mud splattered black pick-up piled so high with goods from the early morning market it seems a rusty cornucopia on wheels. Such overwhelming abundance manages to steal from things their utilitarian identities, their accustomed names and tags—oil, apple, egg, etc. I spy a load of small round red and a bag of long soft green, a mound of fine black, a box of tufted brown, a single waxy yellow ellipse—the whole catalogue from which *maya* chooses to salt-and-sweetly slay the senses. Instantly a dozen or more people pour out of the restaurant. It's as if the entire cast of that play in perpetual progress had been urgently summoned for an unexpected curtain call. They dart across the street, dueling and dodging the steady stream of traffic—a parade of shirtless little boys and giggling girls, barefoot cooks and bored waiters, casual young men who smoke and spit, pregnant women who smile in mysterious exhaustion, the defiant old widow who's been exposing her deflated breasts to gawking tourists for as long as I can remember, even that thousand year old dog that pretends to guard the roadside kitchen door with its limp and its long reliable strand of lukewarm drool. Back and forth they cross and re-cross the busy street for the next ten minutes, graciously accepting their bouquets, their burdens—soft red long green fine black tufted brown waxy yellow—all balanced on heads and shoulders and hips—coming and going and returning until the black pick-up truck, empty at last, screeches into gear and speeds off down the street honking a hole in traffic until it disappears. The kitchen door swings shut. My plate of fried breakfast rice arrives. Act three. Scene forever.

THE ICE ON THE GLASS OF THAT WINDOW

8 June, 1994—Kuta, Bali—

"Don't escape to grieve," I was advised by a friend—and so I left that grief at home. But not, it turns out, that window full of winter storm beside the deathbed—neither the frost on the pane, nor the ceaseless falling of flakes crossing that patch of sky visible between buildings frozen into place on the far side of the ice-cold glass. That view I brought along with me. And it does not melt. Lying here beside me—as close to the line of surf as possible, baking in the delirious heat of the sun—the ice on the glass of that window retains its quiet crystal clarity, despite the sweat that pours from every inch of my skin and washes everything else away.

THE SILKS

9 June, 1994—Kuta, Bali—

Stretched out on my bed beneath the spiral of air stirred by the ceiling fan, the thin billowing silk of my paisley shorts is a delicious complement to the equally thin sting of my sunburnt skin—the silk of pleasure caressing the silk of pain. Oh! The silks! The silks! How shall I ever master renunciation? It's the very thinness of all sensation that makes its play of empty shadows so irresistibly beautiful. I guess I'm doomed to return in my next incarnation as a pair of panties or a handkerchief—my pale blue or deep green silk fading as I hang, forgotten for years, on a clothesline in the brutal sun of this corrupt and lovely world.

FACING THE HUGE ROSE WINDOW
IN THE EAST

12 June, 1994—Kuta, Bali—

I keep returning to the itinerary from my Gothic Cathedral Tour, that document which I scribbled down in the car while navigating to Paris a couple of months ago, driving through the cold rainy spring that followed close on the heels of the icy winter of J's death. The idea was to record just enough detail to tweak memory into doing what it does second-best, remembering—forgetting being its premiere talent . . .

. . . I *had* forgotten that dreamlike Easter Sunday service at Chartres where the words of the liturgy almost got in the way of the more tangible shimmer of physical ritual—the haze of dizzyingly sweet incense; the cover of the closed scripture, the color of dried blood, kissed with passionately closed lips and then held aloft; the live branches so achingly green, dipped in holy dew, then shaken in repeated cloud-bursts over the heads of the assembly; the nervous intoxication of the young novice who I'd seen confessing the day before like Faust in a long black cape, saved from suicide once again by the thrilling pageant of resurrection. I sat facing the huge rose window in the east, brilliantly illuminated by direct morning sunlight and by the joint I'd smoked before breakfast. Its colors were almost too bright for vision to bear. Outside, flocks of birds approached and landed and took flight again—the fluttering of their wings releasing a ghost of trembling shadowplay within the glowing reds and blues and greens and golds of the glass. Were they thieves—flying off with scraps of brilliant color caught in their beaks, dismantling the window? Or were they delivering the colors, constructing the window bit by bit like Cinderella's glass dress? One thing was certain. They were flying off with bits of me. They were flying off with bits of all those who stared into the window's circle of bright flame—the gaze of every eye passing through the stained glass as through a prism of spirit, then taking wing on the far side, soaring off to latitudes and longitudes of unprecedented elasticity.

SAINT NAKED

18 June, 1994—Kuta, Bali—

I've been reading (in Heinrich Zimmer's vast compendium of Indian philosophies) about the Jainist holy men, ascetics who were so idealistic in their worldly pessimism that they carried their devout non-violence to the atomic level—. Don't bruise the air atoms by fanning them when you're overheated! Don't hurt the water atoms by shaking perspiration from the skin, or flailing at the poor defenseless H2O when you fall overboard and find that you're drowning! Seeking to reduce their involvement with matter to a minimum they roamed about with neither destination nor clothes—. Lo and behold! Who should appear this morning on one of the busier streets in this chaotic network of busy streets, but a completely naked wildman out for an afternoon stroll. I've seen this guy for years, usually tattered and shirtless, but never stripped of absolutely everything. Lean and dirty and barefoot, with beautiful dark hollows of eyes and tiny soot smudged nipples, he's always muttering intently to himself, always walking with slow stiff-legged strides right in the middle of traffic. And now unexpectedly there is this dark bird's nest with its pair of pale eggs jiggling between his legs—upon which every eye (both tourist and native) is nervously focused. I picture him very small, in black and white, in pen and ink—an illustration alongside the appropriate word and its definition in the dictionary.

BRUSHSTROKES

19 June, 1994—Kuta, Bali—

for Bill Rice

I see four impossibly handsome young brassiere salesmen walking down the road in burning hot sun, stopping with their wares at one little open-air shop after another—each one balancing an enormous mountain of snow-white brassieres on his shoulder, each one so radiant that I am tempted to stop and buy a few myself just for the pleasure of watching their dark eyes and white teeth flash from the center of each swift shy smile. I walk on down the street, turning back a few minutes later for a last glimpse. Four snow covered peaks rise up weightless through the distant haze of heat. Four simple strokes, bright white, in the painting of a master watercolorist drunk with the casual insanity of the whole wide world caught and cooled at the tip of his brush.

MISGUIDED TOUR

20 June, 1994—Mama's Bavarian Restaurant, Kuta, Bali—

I order some chicken stew topped with something the word for which I can't translate on the menu and the reality of which I can't swallow on the plate. Not to mention the indigestible equatorial German beer-hall music and the blue gingham aprons that match the tablecloths, stains and all. From my seat on the concrete second floor balcony, next to a row of deformed geraniums through which mosquitoes cavort, I can look all the way down *Jalan Legian* buzzing with motorbikes, blinking with low rent neon. Everyone seems to be having a good time! And in a sudden burst of misanthropic altruism I wish I could offer all of them, each and every one, a mouthful or maybe even two of my Bavarian Chicken Stew—and just be done with it. Hours later (my stomach still arguing with lumps of untranslatable topping) small loud children on holiday are screeching their vacation demands to their parents in the bungalow adjacent to mine. I lay on my back on my bed doing nothing for a long time—until both chicken and children are asleep, until the distant boom and tremor of the surf can be heard just beneath the warm slightly salty stillness of another long lean dark night.

A TRAFFIC OF BEES

24 June, 1994—Kuta, Bali—

Only a few months ago on my cathedral pilgrimage commemorating J's death, I stood in the ruins of the abbey at Jumierge, in France, studying a traffic of bees hurrying to and from a hive hidden between the stones of one bleached chapel wall still standing in a field vibrant with spring's green, with sun, and with wind. A flock of dark crows fleeing an abandoned tower swooped and cackled overhead—a black burn against the blue burn of heaven. I remember feeling dizzy for a moment. The earth was turning too furiously beneath me. The air was embroidered with too many different flights—birds and bees and ghosts of centuries of prayer pouring forth from this old stone house-of-cards long since fallen—all these visible and invisible wings brushing against me with such force that I found I had to lean against this one lone high hollow wall filled with whole histories of the hidden honey.

Months have passed. I've crossed the equator. J's ashes have settled into the earth, an earth which turns more slowly now to the rhythm of my ceiling fan. The sun has just settled out beyond the horizon, its infinite ember refusing to cool. I sit quite still, staring at nothing, and listening to—what? Call it a ringing in the ears. Call it a hum, a hiss and crackle of voices haunting my head, a buzzing in my brain. I'd say I was a bee's nest of feelings—if that didn't imply some of the orderliness of the hive.

LOW TIDE

25 June, 1994—Kuta, Bali—

I might never have reached that point had the tide not been so low—uncovering vast tracts of hard packed surf slammed sand, allowing me to skirt the leering faces of the big hotels which are too busy feigning amusement as they stare out to sea to notice the brief passage of brief little me. Just keep walking, I tell myself. Keep walking. Keep walking—if one walks long enough one pops through a wound in the perimeter and finds oneself undeniably elsewhere. It's only that desperate double strand of barbed wire guarding the weed-choked boundaries of the airport that finally stops me in my tracks. Half-buried in a sandbank clustered with wind splintered heat splashed palms is the rusted hull of a small abandoned aircraft. Two naked children straddle the wreck, riding it like a horse—while a third has crawled inside and is beating the rotting metal as if it were a drum. They don't notice me. They don't feel the need in this desolate realm to keep an eye out for meddlesome strangers. I almost convince myself that the world has ended sometime during my long walk, that the big hotels I passed by hours earlier have already been evacuated, both guests and staff exterminated. But then on my way home I pass Father Time himself. A shirtless man carrying an abacus under one impossibly thin arm—he's limping down the street just like me, exhausted, yet still counting.

CROSSED LINES

27 June, 1994—Kuta, Bali—

Where am I—? I seem more and more to be caught in the pages of my journal, in days already passed, in that fantastic series of French Gothic cathedrals visited and recorded there a few months ago. If I stand up and look at myself, naked, in the mirror beside my bed—my skin is a tropic brown, my beard bleached reddish by equatorial sun. Yet if I lay back down on the bed and lose sight of myself, for even a moment, I might end up back on that rocky hilltop of Laon, circling its haunted cathedral during the unforeseen hailstorm that wrestled with my scarf, unbuttoned my jacket, and reddened the little strips of wrist where my sleeves didn't quite reach to the edges of the pockets in which my gloveless hands were seeking shelter. Suddenly I remember how that whole trip began! L and I were sitting in the airport watching two children, twin boys, playing with the receivers of a row of telephones banked against one wall of the departure lounge. They'd pick them up one by one, have a brief imaginary conversation (just like they'd seen adults do), and then hang up again—hurrying on to answer the next phone which was but wasn't really ringing. They were not, however, very careful about putting the receivers back onto those particular cradles where they'd found them. When their parents finally summoned them—telling them to *sit down!* and *behave!*—the boys left behind such a chaos of crossed lines—it's no wonder, all these months later, that I'm still a bit confused as to just where it is that I am.

ZAPPING THE CLOSED LIDS WITH PURE GOLD

26 July, 1994—New York City—

for Leon Sauke

With L and some others, I am fleeing or urgently adventuring though a back-alley landscape of interlocking or overlapping yards and empty lots. At the same time, I am home in New York City having an extraordinary dream. We come to one house whose fence we must leap and whose porch we must scamper across. There is a very old woman living there, and she and her husband *treat* us (that is the word they use) with some sort of machine—a heavy hand-held zapper (that's how I describe it when I scribble it down in my notebook in the middle of the night). They *treat* our faces, touching them lightly with the machine's cool flat nozzle, massaging them with an electrical energy. And then we go on running through the hidden side of landscape—back track back alley back lot, back stage perhaps. Suddenly I am struck in the face by some sort of metal canister that bursts on contact, and drenches me! A moment later, in shock, I see policemen running and surmise that it was a tear-gas canister and that we have blundered on to the scene of a riot. It seems to me to be the back streets of a small seaside tourist town through which my companions now disperse in fear and confusion—leaving me alone with my face and eyes dripping and burning.

I flee back now. I retrace my steps. The police are swarming up ahead as the riot turns more and more violent. I wind up back at the house of the elderly woman and her husband, where I hide in the back seat of an old rusty car abandoned in a field of weeds out beyond their back porch. The woman and her husband offer me a damp cloth with which to wipe the sting from my injured face. I ask if my face has reddened and they say, '*Only your eyes*'—implying that my previous treatment with the electrical machine had probably nullified the potentially more harmful effects of what might not really be tear gas after all. They add, '*We would like to give you another treatment—THIS TIME WITH GOLD!*"

They are enthusiastic experimental doctors and the machine is hauled out once more, heavy as a power tool, with two large round smooth metal plates which rotate like flat mysteriously animated showerheads. They treat each of my eyes, zapping the closed lids with pure gold. Instantly the burning sensation ceases. My vision is soothed, sweetened. They continue on with their work, polishing the skin of my entire face once, ahhhhh—. '*Again,*' one of them insists—. Twice, ahhhhhhh—. My face feels so beautifully relaxed, but I'm afraid that if they repeat the process a third time I might be poisoned by an excess of infused gold. So, they stop. I'm grateful and calm. And I wake—my travels momentarily at an end.

1995

THE SIMPLEST
OF DEW-HARVESTING RECIPES

Open up eternal lips
And swallow me.
Free fallin' through the abyss,
That's where I wanna be.

Michael Hurley

ISLAND

12 May, 1995—Pulau, Micronesia—

for Brad Gaeddert

I'm looking out the window in restless desperation after over 24 hours of almost continual flight, watching the high drama of clouds backlit by low gold sun, watching what appear to be rain showers—long wet wavering filaments, long gray graceful funnels and tunnels, tornados of a darker light dropping down from jagged ridges of gilded cloud into the bare blue of the sea so many miles below. The pilot's voice crackles over the loudspeaker, his stiff Brit upper lip inspiring confidence, neutralizing turbulence. He refers to himself as Ship's Captain. *"Due to severe storms in the area our landing has been delayed. In the meantime, ladies and gentlemen, I thought we might circle the island at our leisure while I point out several of the smaller adjacent islands favored by local and professional divers."* The plane tilts dramatically. My square little window is suddenly flooded with infinite sea—a contour map of blue deeps and blue shallows and what look like brilliant blue continents submerged below crystal blue depths. And then the little eruptions of fur-or-forest-covered coral—as if someone has scattered a handful of earth's seeds which are only just beginning to sprout from the surface of this watery waste. Twenty minutes later we head down, into rain, and everything grows darker and darker (including the interior of the plane) as we sink first into drenched cloud, and then emerge into lush green haze, finally touching down onto hard gray rain-slicked pavement alongside a tiny wet white building—a toy house with a peaked roof of soggy thatch and eaves of dark unfinished wood. We're told to remain in our seats while tanks are re-fueled and the tiny onboard kitchen is re-stocked with a few hundred tasteless sandwiches packaged in little red and white cardboard boxes for a last mid-air picnic, some hours later, before reaching our final destination. But by then, I am convinced, our final destination has already come and gone. It has been left far behind. For months afterwards I will be reluctant to look at a map, preferring to believe that the mysterious island of storm will *not* appear there—that it is just one more of the unrecoverable details, the lost moments of a life in perpetual motion littered with expired airplane tickets and the stale and tasteless crusts of half-eaten, high-altitude sandwiches.

THE RELEVANT SACRAMENT

14 May, 1995—Kuta, Bali—

Another stray dog collapsed in public, on the final threshold—pressed flat on its stomach, body skeletal—chin resting in its own clear vomit, which leaks weakly from its mouth, draining away with what is left of its life. What exactly is it that is demanded at such a moment of the practitioner of compassion? What external or internal gesture? A pat on the head. A tidbit of food. A brief burst of indignation at callous passers-by. *These* would seem to be clearly beside the point, and much too far after the fact. Acknowledgment of The Fact—. That would appear to be the only relevant sacrament remaining—. The inner voice that says, "Ah yes, this is it, this is the moment of death." The moment (as William James put it) in which *every individual existence goes out in a lonely spasm of helpless agony.* He goes on. *If you protest, my friend, wait till you arrive there yourself.* And so I nod my brief and sober farewell to Sam Beckett's dying dog, and carry on, forward, toiling, toward my own faithful final threshold—everyman's best friend.

MY BATHROOM

17 May, 1995—Petulu, Bali—

The western wall is tiled in pale blue, with a cracked blue sink, a blue toilet, and a mirror—all overhung with a slant of thatch. The eastern side is roofless, bounded by a rough rock wall enclosing an always dripping garden of ferns and hanging orchids and a twisted wild rose bush which I have never witnessed in bloom. One half of the floor is tiled. The other half, the garden ground, is spread with ordinary stones that sing under footsteps or raindrops. There's a shower head jutting from one of the walls that joins east and west—which is perfect because I always feel all wet when I'm half in one world and half in another. What a treat to sit on the toilet and wipe my ass while watching the moon rise through the palms, or to walk directly from warm shower into cool rain.

LIVING POWDER

25 May, 1995—Petulu, Bali—

I watch the gecko that lives in my roof thatch catch and eat a large confused moth. Halfway through its meal a pale patterned fragment of a wing comes floating through the air, descending to earth—part dismembered angel, part autumn leaf. It lands at the foot of my bed, followed by a few grains of living powder—a glitter of untranslatable dust delivered, sparkling, by the ghost that haunts the dream of a beam of clear moon light.

BUTTERFLY NOTES

28 May, 1995—Petulu, Bali—

In the bowels of an antique shop of questionable pedigree, I pick up a relic from a lower shelf reeking of rat and spider: a long thin unpainted figure of a woman—melancholy, kneeling. I point to the pattern engraved in the wood, beneath the breasts, above the bended knees. *"Kupu-kupu?"* I ask. *"Butterfly?"* Several people within earshot giggle as it is pointed out to the foreigner that the butterfly in question is the woman's vagina, hovering between her dusty wooden legs. Clearly there are butterflies everywhere here—not only in the garden, harassing hibiscus, a-tango with hummingbirds—but in dusty dark old junk shops as well. Just last night at a dance in a local village they were aflutter before me in the guise of two adolescent girls—cocooned in gilt cloth and decorated with fresh-picked frangipani blossoms, each slender wrist graced with a restlessly glittering golden wing.

ORNITHOLOGY

1 June, 1995—Petulu, Bali—

for Jeanne Hedstrom

1.

Yesterday morning during the first half of my first cup of coffee, I sat listening to the *Seldom-Seen Silver-Hammered Early Bird.* Rumor has it—a rumor I intend to start—that it remains invisible even when caught and caged, and that it builds its noisy nest from old lost coins which it 'hammers' into a sort of shallow teacup without a handle. Needless to say, it is most commonly heard in secluded areas where pirates' treasure is reputedly buried. While all the other early birds are busy fussing with their worms, this one is busy feathering its nest with gold and silver doubloons.

2.

The *Yellow-Bellied Broom-Tailed Leaf Abuser* is somewhat of a pest, except for the fact that it invariably sweeps up after its debauchery—hence all these neat little piles of leaf scraps which one chances upon along the garden's paths.

3.

Mistaking the glimmer of sunlight upon the surface of any body of water (be it sea or lake or puddle) for a rare blossom, the *Shiny Shallow Sunbird* spends its brief life-span stabbing for reflected nectar, for false gems and fool's gold—its long sharp beak invariably coming up dripping and empty. More popularly known as the *Doomed Water-Diamond Bird*, it rarely lives for more than a few months—starving to death when quite young, or drowning in frustration. How it reproduces remains to this day an unsolved mystery—a mystery which has given rise to a substantial body of abstruse ornithological speculation as to the potency of illusion.

4.

The *Reckless Honey-Bearded Water Buzzard*, an excellent diver, can plunge straight through the center of a beehive—escaping (due to its great strength and speed) unscathed, unstung, dripping honey. However, such dramatic aerial acrobatics require subsequent dives of equal vehemence into water—for the remnants of the sticky honey *must* be rinsed from its feathers before it dries, cementing them together and making it impossible for the bird to fly. On the whole, a tragic bird—its ecstatic feats of flight rewarded by an infinite sweetness, as well as by an often-pathetic death. No one who has seen a *Reckless Honey-Bearded Water Buzzard* stuck fast to the ground, covered with ants, breathing its last—will ever forget the sight. Its shrieking cry, at such times, is almost indistinguishable from that which it utters as it dives, insatiable, through the hive.

SALT UNDER STARS

2 June, 1995—Petulu, Bali—

for S Again

In the *Mutus Liber,* the *Mute Book* of alchemy in which the entire secret of the Art is illustrated without a single word, the Great Work begins with a rather laborious collection of dew. A man and a woman set out squares of cloth on the grass overnight, and at dawn they wring them out over a basin—with great effort gathering night's manna-from-heaven. All this is done under the sign of Aries—spring being the season in which the *prima materia* sacrifices itself in its perfect infancy. I have accidentally stumbled upon a different recipe for the collection of dew, one which eliminates the need for cumbersome cotton cloths and copper basins and aching laundry-muscles. There is a little saucer of salt which remains on my porch table after all the other breakfast dishes have been cleared away. It remains there all afternoon, all evening, all night. Each dawn I wake to find this small saucer full of dew-drenched salt—salt saturated up to, but not past, the point of dissolution. I have leapt to the wholly poetic conclusion that not only does the salt attract (like blades of grass) the cold sweat of the stars to earth—but that there is a dew hidden in salt to begin with, a latent dew—. Mine is the simplest of dew-harvesting recipes, a boon and a blessing to the overworked alchemist: LEAVE SALT OUT UNDER STARS. ABANDON AND SERVE.

OPEN VEIN

4 June, 1995—Petulu, Bali—

According to Hindu myth there was a great sage and ascetic named Rsi Mankanaka whose superhuman austerities performed in his deep-forest hermitage caused plant sap to flow in his veins, thus releasing him from the bondage of blood. One day he cut his finger—and seeing the fern juice or hibiscus nectar or laurel or maple milk or syrup oozing from the wound, he rejoiced! He tumbled into an ecstatic organic trance, and began to dance so blissfully that the very fabric of the universe threatened to unravel. It seemed more than creation could bear! Worried gods appealed in desperation to the power of Siva. Siva came to the forest to witness Rsi Mankanaka's dance of freedom. Standing erect before the ecstatic yogi, Siva opened his own veins. A tide of white powder poured forth which stopped Rsi Mankanaka in mid-step. So free was Siva from all attachments and bondages, both bloody and otherwise, that his veins ran with nothing but ash—pale weightless ash, the ultimate residue of the realm of manifestation. Then Siva danced! And the venerable vegetable yogi, well, he prostrated himself (as I imagine it) like a leaf still bowed down with moisture after a violent rainstorm.

SANCTUARY

20 June, 1995—Petulu, Bali—

I am reading the newspaper on the porch in the pouring rain,
an editorial in the New York Herald Tribune written by Toby
Thompson which contains the following sentence— *"It is written
that Medieval Europeans drove stakes through the hearts of suicides,
to thwart their afterlives as vampires, then buried them at a
crossroads where the weight of footsteps would dampen their rage..."*
I look up from the page of print, eyes crossing the porch to
where a bewildered butterfly is fluttering about under the eaves,
seeking refuge from the storm. I try to welcome it—yet within
moments it has deserted me, preferring a single broad leaf out in
the wet garden beneath which to shelter from the driving rain.
Perched upside down, it waits patiently for the sun to come out.
But the sun does not come out. Once in a while the butterfly
opens and closes its black and yellow wings with what seems a
soft sigh.

1996

IN THE SUBLUNARIUM

*But as darkness thickened a weird thing happened
which I cannot describe. It was as if some torn pages
from a marvelous story were blown by a sudden
spring breeze to flutter around the various rooms
of that vast palace. They could be followed so far,
but never right to the end. I spent my nights wandering
from room to room chasing those swirling torn pages.*

Rabindranath Tagore

JUNE 20 JUNE 20

20 June, 1996—Petulu, Bali—

First, sixteen hours of dense and dreamless sleep. Then I settle down on the porch, open my journal and, as I date this entry, notice that the month and the day match last year's last entry exactly—except for the year, of course. Enclosed in that circle, I sit flipping and flapping backwards through the pages that lie before me and yet behind me, deciphering last year's scrawl and the year's before that and the year's before that—chasing my own tail, tortured by the delights of memory.

An hour after escaping from the airport, gazing out the window of the van carrying me up north, I saw a hat in the middle of the road. A few yards ahead a motorcycle had come to a dead halt, stopping traffic, or at least diverting it—as a boy who couldn't have been more than nine or ten years old ran back to retrieve what had been lost in the wind.

THE HANDLE OF THE PLOW ITSELF

22 June, 1996—Petulu, Bali—

An old farmer is out plowing this afternoon with an infernal contraption made of red-hot screws, muddy pitchfork prongs, and rusty saw blades—all held together with the stench and screech of burning rubber and rancid petrol. And not one sweet tired old brown cow in sight. Indeed, the brutally heavy wooden collar traditionally used to yoke oxen here would seem a lovely lace ruff in comparison to this damned machine—which seems to be dragging the old man up and down each furrow, instead of the other way around. Across the muddy *sawah,* far beyond the noise of progress, stands a small shrine to *Dewi Sri,* the rice goddess—a stone tower with a little open window for offerings, topped with a ragged yellow flag flapping casually up to god in the wind. The urban westerner's romantic perspective poses the crucial questions—will the goddess deign to descend to the shrine? Or will the din of machinery make her feel unwelcome? Is it only beasts of burden that are capable of worship? More practical rural realists, they who actually pull the plow right off the postcard, the Balinese will no doubt leave their scraps of proffered petal and leaf and their sticky grains of boiled rice not only within the designated inner sanctum of the shrine of harvest, but also upon the handle of the plow itself—before it begins to cough and spit and growl—or afterwards, its overheated motor lying exhausted and idle in ancient mud.

IN THE SUBLUNARIUM

30 June, 1996—Petulu, Bali—

Sleeping has become so hard to resist here—far from the closed air and the odor of human curry in my New York City tenement apartment, here in my mosquito net cathedral of spider web and wandering faery spittle, cool air everywhere embroidered with frogs and crickets and geckos calling. By the time the sun sinks and the temperature drops from burning to balmy and then to downright cool, it's no wonder I can't resist diving straight down into deep sleep for another nine or ten hours of compulsive sublunary circus act. That circus is escalating at an alarming rate—its rings multiplying like ripples in disturbed water, its clowns and its acrobats growing more and more brazen. Already I've had a dream about a pair of beautiful large dangling turquoise earrings, and another about a documentary filmmaker named Bill Collins Russell who was known for his legendary remark, "Oh no! Now I'll have to film that too!" In that same dream autumn leaves turned into pale elbow macaronis and there was a Soviet conspiracy to suppress heart attack statistics. The night before last found me creeping through other people's backyards like when I was a child, several times climbing over the wrought iron fences of major museums. I hardly remember last night's dreams—but at some point an insane person was sitting bound with thin white ropes in a crisscross pattern in the middle of the rice fields through which I went out walking yesterday alone and awake. Either he couldn't escape, or he refused to budge.

TAKING A BROOM TO THE STARS

1 July, 1996—Petulu, Bali—

All night I am moving into a new house of dreams—sweeping up, clearing out, getting lost in unfamiliar rambling rooms. There are bright tiny scraps of adhesive paper that have to be brushed from the dark wooden paneling of the walls—it's like taking a broom to the stars, like rearranging one's horoscope—. And there was rain last night, the first since I've been here. Not a heavy rain, but a rain light and steady, just enough to draw a persistent whisper from the palms outside in the garden. And just enough of a breeze to stir my mosquito netting, to make it breathe, to make it billow all night long like the hem of a passing ghost or a cloud changing shape. It's all behind me now, I think upon waking—everything's been smoothed, the past swept clean, the present a pleasant dream.

MASK

3 July, 1996—Mas, Bali—

The epileptic boy who B helped years ago—taking him to a doctor in Denpasar, a specialist who prescribed a medicine which proved moderately effective—has since died. I learn this from the owner of the shop behind which B and I had first caught sight of him sitting in the dirt and drooling—ignored by those around him like a sick stray dog. B paid for the medicine, of course. It was relatively expensive, a true taste of luxury for this poor boy—a brief respite from painful fits of convulsion and confusion. B has since left Bali. The owner of the shop still wears a thick mask of pancake make-up on her face presumably to disguise some blemish, some embarrassing skin condition. She is very sweet, very friendly, and speaks very matter-of-factly about the boy. "He grew very thin," she tells me, "and then he died." She shakes her head just a little bit from side to side. *"Susa,"* she pronounces—*"Pity."*

CROSSING THE PERFORMER'S LINE

4 July, 1996—Petulu, Bali—

I am a member of a dance troupe all of whom are wanted by the police. After being chased for a long time, we find ourselves at the scene of a great open-air performance, pursued right up onto the stage before a waiting audience. Having thus crossed the performer's line, the police are unable to follow us further and we start dancing immediately. Upon waking, I still remembered vividly the song to which we'd danced. It seemed familiar, a classic swing tune that I recognized—yet I couldn't quite recall the name of it. And now, hours later, I've lost the words and the music as well. Though I did jot down a partial lyric before it faded—something about a missing radio and a hot water bottle. The performance itself was pure spectacle, one of those cast-of-thousands all-singing all-dancing movie musical numbers that takes place unbelievably in the great outdoors—a mythic Oklahoma, Hoboken, Tahiti, or old Shanghai—all the native inhabitants joining in as preposterous extras. I wonder how many of us dancers ended up in jail.

THE SEA WILL RECEIVE

5 July, 1996—Kuta, Bali—

The tourists are often surprised. Vague rumblings of ritual's approach have reached them—but without any active desire on their part to ferret out its details, such details are not forthcoming from the locals. Near-naked oily Westerners are suddenly grabbing for their gaudy towels and double-duty vacation sarongs, running for cover before the rising tide of ceremony. The grand procession appears: women bearing on their heads huge pyramids of fruit, men shouldering enormous bronze gongs, and two giant puppets lurching from side to side like Mr. and Mrs. Beanstalk in a vaguely menacing fairy tale. Hundreds of Balinese gather for seaside purification with a casual seriousness that falls mercifully short of the solemnity of a crucified Christ's more claustrophobic cleansing back home.

There *is* ritual in sunbathing, I suppose—a sort of seaside purification *is* hard at work there as well. Thus there is a meeting of two rituals here, this afternoon—the sacred and the secular encountering one another at the lip of the world, at the edge of the island of earth they share. And when it is all over a few hours later, mysteriously deliberate mounds of intricately woven palm fronds and wild flower petals and banana slices and sticky rice are left behind, alongside whatever remains of a tourist's afternoon at the beach—empty soda cans and plastic water bottles, maybe an orphaned wristwatch, or a used mass market paperback thriller, its cover bleached and badly torn. And whatever the gods and the dogs can't dispose of, the sea will receive, be it sacred or profane—for the sea makes no such distinctions.

113

IT'S A DARK HOUSE

There is an opening downward within each moment,
an unconscious reverberation, like the thin thread
of the dream that we awaken with in our hands each morning
leading back and down into the image of the dark.
                                        —James Hillman

                          6 July, 1996—Kuta, Bali—

As I fumble hurriedly, preparing pen and paper, the dream's first
scene slips from my memory—leaving only a single phrase with
no *dramatis personae* or plot attached: *DON'T WORRY IT'S A*
DARK HOUSE. I don't even know if this sentence refers to the
dream at all. If there *was* a dark house I have forgotten it, though
I like to think that I *would* recognize it if I found myself upon its
threshold again. In the dream's second scene, hastily recorded in
a nearly illegible scrawl, I am in a boat with my brother and some
others. My brother falls overboard—not because of any mishap
or misstep of his own—but due to some playful commotion on
board. '*Shenanigans*' was the word I scribbled down. '*The sins of*
the family' is the phrase that comes to mind now. Perhaps that's
when I say—"Don't worry. It's a dark house."

I throw my brother an orange nylon rope. At first, he fails to
catch hold of it. I can see it coiling eel-like just beneath the
surface of the water, an electric worm in the dull green and gray
murk. Circling back, taking a fresh approach, the rope of rescue
is tossed once again—and this time I see his hand flashing in the
water like a fish taking the orange bait. I gesture affirmatively
with my eyes and chin, without word or sound. As we swing
round again, the rope growing taut, I begin to speak at last—
instructing him to *pull, pull, pull* upon the rope which is fastened
to an iron cleat on one side of our vessel—until the boat is
pulled *by* him, *to* him, and he clambers aboard at last. Yet I have
the distinct feeling that the whole sequence of events happens

twice—or is that duplication effected only by my efforts to remember? When replayed in my mind there seems to be a dark dock, a ledge or a single step to assist his re-entry into the boat. And right before he rises up out of the water that second time there is a moment of panic on my part—no—not panic—more a moment of morbid curiosity. Perhaps, it occurs to me, when he emerges he'll be missing a leg, perhaps he'll be invisible from the waist down—like the victim in one of those terror-tales who is so numbed by shock and freezing water that he does not even feel the shark's attack. Or perhaps, I now fantasize calmly—for this is no nightmare—he has sacrificed his legs to the *dark house* of water, legs which are still pacing round, torso-less, far below the surface.

STILL POOR A LITTLE BIT

7 July, 1996—Kuta, Bali—

Last night in a twisted heap on the bare hot pavement of a thriving tourist thoroughfare, dropped down to the floor of the forest of scurry where the view is all tanned ankles and plastic sandals, I see my old crippled beggar friend once again. He almost doesn't recognize me at first—it *has* been several years—but when he does, he gets so excited that he almost hugs me, his scrawny misshapen arms flailing about unselfconsciously like strands of tangled seaweed waving underwater. To celebrate such a special occasion, I graduate at long last from coins to paper money—. I can't be bothered to count—. I simply empty my pocket—. *'Bapak masih tidak kaya?'* I ask. 'Father still no rich?' *'Masih miskin sidikit,'* he replies—his metal teeth, a tarnished mouthful of them, flashing in the headlamps of a passing motorbike as he smiles. 'Still poor a little bit.'

SHAPES SUFFICIENT TO GUIDE ME

8 July, 1996—Kuta, Bali—

Suddenly all the electricity goes off. I have no candle. And for the first ten minutes or so, until my eyes adjust to purest black, I am suspended in the nowhere that the elsewhere of travel is only a preliminary taste of. I am frozen, yes—. Yet sweating nonetheless—. Beneath the paralyzed ceiling fan, I am waiting for black to turn to gray, for shapes to return, shapes sufficient to guide me across the room, through the door, outside—where the refuge of starlight lessens the impact of night. So it is that the little deaths prepare us for the larger: sleep, darkness, disappointment, electrical failure, apocalypse, and the tremulous mirage of the suffering of others viewed from an uncertain distance.

Before I left the mountains for the coast, Wayan confided in me. He told me that a friend of his from the village (someone I know casually as a humble and mild-mannered man of few unnecessary words) grew so troubled and confused by financial and family obligations that he stabbed himself seven times in the chest with what was no doubt the dull knife of a perpetually difficult life. He did not die, of course, but was merely forced to figure out a way to pay for his exorbitantly expensive stay in a second-or-third-rate hospital.

Suddenly all the electricity comes back on.

SAINT SHARK ATTACK

10 July, 1996—Petulu, Bali—

1.

I bear witness to a man beneath the surface of some sea who is about to use a weapon against one of two underwater companions. He's already loaded his gun with a long sharp spear and is about to aim and fire—when suddenly he is distracted by less fathomable dangers and, in a panic, casts his eyes down into water's infinite depths. At *that* moment his eyes become mine. I see a shark approaching. I see its head looming, the mouth a ring of sharp teeth opening and closing like a lethal anemone, gaping wider and wider as it advances closer and closer. Yet because I am not really the character in the dream, but merely looking out through *his* eyes, merely listening as to *his* vivid story—I am not terrified but only calmly appalled by this frightful specter, this awful beast of the deep. As in a graceful underwater ballet, the shark strikes. And as the spilled blood begins to seep into the sea in that peculiar way that two liquids have of meeting and merging, the man, whose name is Dominic, bends further and further forward in order to suck the blood from his wounded foot—until he is floating in pale pink bloodstained water like the circular alchemical emblem of the dragon swallowing its own tail.

2.

The story resumes much later when Dominic, having taken monastic vows, has all but disappeared from public life. He has been warned by the powers that be about the dangers of growing too *fat* or too *poor* like other celebrated monks who have undergone the same painful ordeal of revelation and conversion—ascetic devotees who have likewise sworn to abandon all effort of any kind. This is when I enter the dream myself. This is when I enter the dream *as* myself. I am in a shabby shadowy room filled with just the sort of overweight indigents that Dominic has been forewarned to avoid the fate of. Someone in tattered ecclesiastical-purple is listlessly plunking coins down onto a wooden tabletop—mostly copper pennies, with the occasional silver dime. Abruptly I sweep the coins with one hand into the palm of the other, several of them falling to the floor and ringing against the flagstones. I look down at them and see, at the same instant, the feet of the assembled monks—each shod with a unique, pathetically worn and ill-fitting pair of pauper's patched shoes. This is the most vivid image of my strange dream: these shabby shoes. I then leave the room without retrieving the escaped pennies that have fallen to the floor. In the hall outside, the character I have become in the dream encounters Dominic for the first time. He is tall, with long thin arms and legs and loose lank hands. He wears a knitted gray or lavender sweater with a few chipped buttons undone at the neck and a stretched-out hem which hangs down unevenly over the tops of his trousers. He has a large round paunch betokening, as per his vow, great physical and material idleness—or laziness as the religiously uninitiated might choose to call it.

3.

The story abruptly becomes a film, fast forwarding to a vision of Dominic's, a vision of the Virgin Mary. I see (for I am back in *his* eyes now) two figures, a man and a woman, who sit back on their knees facing one another. Their arms are raised and in their hands they are holding replicas of each other's heads in such a way that they can stare into each other's eyes while the heads which they hold aloft can do likewise. Slowly they shift the position of these hand-held heads—moving them slightly to one side and tipping them down so that the disembodied eyes can gaze now into the eyes of those heads still attached—thus achieving a circulatory system of eye contacts whose parameters and purpose and whose relation to the Virgin Mother escapes me the moment I awake. I arise and untuck the edges of my mosquito net and gather it up into a little white knot over the bed. As I am writing down the hagiographic details of the dream of the Legend of Saint Dominic, I glance up suspiciously at the knot of net which hangs over my abandoned sheets and wrinkled pillow like a small cumulus cloud withholding rain.

CONCLUDING WITH A MAGIC TRICK

16 July, 1996—Kuta, Bali—

School starts. I and my friend P are both taking a course taught by a renegade film director. First project—*construct a small drama that incorporates one half of a sphere of polished lapis lazuli or map agate.* Mine takes the shape of a love story which concludes with a magic trick by means of which everything is resolved blissfully: I hold the half-stone-sphere in one hand placed mysteriously behind my back, I squeeze it into my tightly closed fist, and then I roll it across the floor—for it has become miraculously round, a simple symbol of love's completion. Later, P is trying to tell me about *his* school project. We are standing atop a structure, an architectural ruin of some sort—high roofless walls upon whose narrow spines we are balanced above deep empty chambers. Or perhaps it is a children's playground, ultra-modern in design. Or an enormous concrete beehive, abandoned. P is complaining about the delay in completing his own little play. He claims it is all because he has unwisely entrusted certain technical details (copying, collating, proof-reading, etc) to a bogus *Literary Agent.* I am sympathetic—but must interrupt to tell him that I am growing increasingly dizzy atop this tall wall and may soon fall or be forced by my vertigo to jump into any available body of water. I am already keeping an emergency eye out for a lake, a river, or the sea.

MAN'S BEST FRIEND AND MAN

18 July, 1996—Kuta, Bali—

I wonder how much longer the old dog at *Made's Warung* can survive. This year it's sporting a huge hairless patch on the left side of its back, a barren field crossed from one end to the other by a mean neon pink path of scar. And yet the old ticker is still keeping time—blocking traffic, shitting thin gruel, sleeping most of the day, keeping time, keeping time, keeping time. Likewise the old guy across the street who, at exactly the same hour each morning—for as long as I can remember—has been hanging up his old faded *hats-for-sale* in the little alleyway that runs from the busy street back to his hidden house. His legs grow thinner and thinner every year. Each knee is like a knot in a taut string. This morning as he moves slowly on, down the line, I watch the hats slipping silently from their bent rusty nails—one at a time, just behind his back, as close on his heels as his own shadow. At the end of line, he turns—and just as placidly, retracing his steps, he picks up the fallen hats, one at a time, with no trace of impatience, dusting them off and hanging them up once more on their bent nails—from which, moments later, they drop yet again, settling soundlessly behind him—pale polyester autumn leaves, their colors bleached by years of sun, marking his path, his past, his future.

THROUGH THE WINDOW OF THE CHAMBER
OF NEUROTIC TORTURES

20 July, 1996—Kuta, Bali—

I am learning smuggling techniques from a man named Mr. Costageña. He's an underworld mobster, a master of violence and profit, in secret control of some society situated far in the future. The dream is set in a familiar place but in an unfamiliar time.

At a large party Mr. Costageña plays a brutal practical joke. Many of the gathered guests are already in on this joke, which is one of their sinister host's favorites—but I am not one of those *in the know.* I have not yet been initiated. He offers me a ring whose gem is a disarmingly anal rubber rose or plastic flower. It looks a lot like one of those cheap gag surprise-squirt rings. He places it ceremoniously upon my finger and carefully adjusts it so that it is facing outward. "Otherwise," he warns, "you'll get it *everywhere!* And I mean *EVERYWHERE!*" Immediately I feel a growing pressure. The tip of my ringed finger begins to ache as if it is swelling. I am afraid to look at it, but am drawn to it at the same time. Finally, my fascination overcomes my fear. I look down. It seems to me that my fingertip is as swollen as a little balloon about to burst. I begin to sweat. I tear the ring off my finger and fling it to the ground. Ha ha ha. Everyone laughs. The joke is on me. For in truth the ring is merely a bit too small, it squeezes only slightly—yet due to the anxiety elicited by Costageña's stern warning, as well as by his general air of recklessly illicit authority, the wearer of the ring invariably anticipates and thus hallucinates a terrible explosion of some sort. Dear Mr. Costageña never fails to find this spectacle hilarious each and every time he orchestrates it.

But there is a window in the cruel comic room. A window through which is visible a miraculous potted plant—*a plant of many wonders.* The plant is in constant metamorphosis. It shoots out long tentacles and filaments that transform themselves from one moment to the next, assuming various shapes and structures which anchor themselves for brief architectural instants (by means of some soft and sticky mechanism of suction) to the glass of the window—and then seconds later they send out new sprouts and shoots, new tentacles, new branches which go on changing and rearranging, dissolving one order into another in a single seamless stream of endless patterns. It is astoundingly beautiful, a wondrous spectacle—and all of a lovely cool green color with flecks of pale blue like foam on agitated water. The dream's focus tries hard to remain inside the room—in the rubber ring of humiliation, in the runaway imagination's neurotic chamber of tortures. At first the plant outside the window is merely scenery glimpsed from the very corner of an eye. The ha ha ha in the room compels me. I turn back to the crime lord and his hyenas several times. But they are ultimately utterly eclipsed by these green snowflakes concretizing on the far side of the glass— blossoming crystals fastening themselves to form, freezing, then melting away again, then returning, ever changing—like molecules in an accelerated matter of infinite beauty. I had the distinct impression in the dream that this plant of wonders had been engineered somehow. In this future society the constant transmutation of things organic had been harnessed—potted like a plant, plugged in like an appliance. And now no home was without one! No matter what scenes of cruelty or confusion or questionable comedy might be taking place indoors, planted outside of every window of every room was one of these strange organic engines of design. I have no idea what happened to Mr. Costageña. I lost all track of him.

TAKE THEM BOTH

21 July, 1996—Kuta, Bali—

I've been reading Ramakrisna's incantatory prayers at bedtime.

To my Divine Mother I prayed only for pure love.
I offered flowers at her Lotus Feet and prayed:
Mother here is Thy virtue, here is Thy vice. Take them both
and grant me only pure love for Thee.
Here is Thy knowledge, here is Thy ignorance. Take them both
and grant me only pure love for Thee.
Here is Thy purity, here is Thy impurity. Take them both
and grant me only pure love for thee.

As I sleep, I hear rumors of a woman who is notorious in certain private circles for taking explicit sado-masochistic photographs of the rich and famous. I know where she lives. I decide to investigate—just to satisfy my curiosity, nothing more than that. I go to her shabby storefront office and have to wait for a very long time due to the fact that she is on the telephone long distance. While I wait, a man enters the office and sits down beside me—waiting also. I begin to talk with him. And as I do, my true intentions for seeking out this woman of nasty rumor become clear to me for the first time. I am here to warn her. I am here to warn her of *another* investigation, one more 'official' and less sympathetic than my own. I tell this man in the waiting room all about my suspicions. And then when the woman hangs up the telephone, I follow her into a private backroom and there confess all of my fears to her as well. I caution her, citing the increasingly conservative climate of the community in which we live, expressing my concern for her safety and continued well-being. Yet through it all she remains unperturbed, unthreatened by sordid revelations of potential persecution.

I offered flowers to her Lotus Feet and prayed . . .

Flowers, sandal-paste, vilwa-leaves, red hibiscus, rice pudding,
and various sweets
and other articles of worship . . .
Here is Thy virtue, here is Thy vice . . .

And here are the photographs, of course.

STOWAWAY FLAME

24 July, 1996—Kuta, Bali—

Mind racing ahead to the next day's departure at dusk, I have trouble sleeping on my last night. Unconscious at long last, I dream that I am already back in Manhattan, already back in my neighborhood bar—just standing around, drinking in old habits. The familiar leisure of the scene however is soon interrupted by one unsettling element: on the back of someone's hand (an anonymous hand) there appears quite guilelessly a tiny opalescent creature—. An ant or a beetle, a miniature reptile, or a tiny crustacean of some sort, I suspect it may have crawled from this stranger's hand onto or into my own. Either that or I am the stranger who's brought it back with me all the way from the tropics—fastened to me like a case of luminous crabs, a radioactive spider in my luggage, a scorpion in my shoe. While I watch, the creature begins to catch fire, one leg at a time flares up and sizzles—crackling audibly. Yet the ant or beetle or reptile or crab or spider or scorpion is neither killed nor consumed. I'm not sure if anyone else present even notices these quick little conflagrations. There is no smell of smoke or smoke alarm, no stench or stain of sulfur. And after several of these bursts of minor flame the creature crawls away unharmed without disrupting business-as-usual at the bar. I'm pretty drunk by the time I awake and begin packing.

THEY HELD MY EYES

25 July, 1996—Kuta, Bali—

An early half-moon in a late afternoon sky of pale blue—just the top half, like a floating skull cap with no face—with only bare blue below. And in that bare blue distance, like dark ciphers, one two three four five six seven kites suspended. I lose myself in thought, time passes, clouds roll in, lightly at first, then more heavily as it begins to rain. With my head tilted back against the porch chair I gaze up at the tops of coconut palms, I place myself amongst the coconuts clustered there—exposed to a rain high above myself. My eyes are distracted, drawn to the single kite, one out of seven, still remaining. I wonder—*how much longer can it keep on flying alone in this rain?* The rain grows heavier, steadier. I watch and I wait. At last the kite begins to sink, straight down—moving at a determined pace as if walking offstage after a classical soliloquy perfectly executed and delivered to an all but empty theatre. Rising from my chair I go inside to finish packing my bags.

When I return to the porch it has stopped raining, the clouds have withdrawn, the blue of the sky has returned, deeper and brighter now, washed unbearably clean. I can't find the moon. Did I imagine it? I look up to see if the kite might still be visible in some quarter of the heavens, and the dark flutter of the wing of a bird fools me for a moment—until the bird settles atop one of those tall coconut palms which had held my eyes for a few graceful moments of rain on an afternoon of departure.

1997

THROUGH THE LOOSENED WEAVE

What were these caves, after all?
Is it not conceivable that after emerging from them,
those troglodytes found themselves
under the starlit celestial vault as if in a larger cave,
but capable, after their experience of interiority,
of extrapolating yet a further outside?

Andre VandenBroek

CROUCHED, GREEN AND LUSTROUS

13 March, 1997—Petulu, Bali—

Fifteen hours in—. A long sleep and a slight toothache, a tepid cup of coffee, and a not-yet-morning musing. In the garden of shadows at 3:30 AM the heart drifts, slipping drowsily from one current of affection to another, making inaudible vows to everyone and everything that has touched it and lingered in memory. The flight was endless, but endurable. A flurry of unlikely last-minute long-distance phone calls in my Manhattan apartment made the echo of departure resonate with heightened drama. Taking leave has become more and more difficult for me as I get older, and then even older—. Each point of embarkation seems of such exaggerated significance, it takes so many days and so many obscure private rituals for me to bid farewell to my old self, that self that I'll never see again once the journey transforms me into someone else. For one never really returns, unless it is all a return and each new voyage is only a stripping away, a shedding of yet another skin.

Now—. Wind in leaves, sunlight on water, waves of someone else's language, all washing over me—my new weather, my new equatorial spinal column, warped slightly like the trunk of a tall palm—is that my brain balanced on top like a young coconut? Hours of pre-dawn darkness, with cold fried rice and cooled coffee, have slowed me down to the point where I can begin my next life here, far away from those frantic pursuits in which I was indulging this past week in the city I've left so far behind. Is the secular Dionysus really the most demanding of the archetypal gods—? No denying the grip of his wine-stained fingers about the base of the cock, a grip so firm one can scarcely dance to his drunken commands. Yet something more virginal is in order now, something quieter—though no less ferocious. I picture a tropical Artemis crouched out in the garden, green and lustrous, like that frog which sat motionless on the path an hour ago,

131

incidentally illuminated by the beam of my flashlight—full of
leap and life, yet not moving a muscle. When the sun finally rises
this morning it will emerge from the cunt of that quiet Queen
of Toads—for this new wilderness is Hers, as am I, for the next
two months.

HANGING IDLE, CARRYING ON

16 March, 1997—Petulu, Bali—

I wonder: is there any particular time of day or night that ants prefer to sleep, or do they work continuously in shifts? I'm watching enormous spiders weaving. They are all long legs, legs busy as old women's knitting needles in elastic slow motion. They are looping and crossing those long sticky threads oozing from the negligible ellipses of their bodies. As always the mischievous child in me cannot keep from vandalizing the web, pitching fruit pits and cracker crumbs into the labyrinth, rending the completed nexus, disillusioning the tirelessly methodical spiders. So thoroughly did I bother one of them that it simply abandoned its web altogether—hanging idle all afternoon from an arc of palm—dangling by one short thread, lethal legs drooping, like the skeleton of a droplet of evaporating water. Beneath it, on the ground—the next shift of ants toiling, carrying on.

HARDBOILED EGGS OF LIGHT

23 March, 1997—Petulu, Bali—

At approximately eight o'clock each morning the sun breaks through a mist, through a lattice of palm frond and banana leaf. It strikes the surface of the little fishpond alongside my porch, and its rays are then reflected off the water and up onto the porch of my bungalow. You know how light dances and glances off water—? How its flicker falls somewhere between the wings of angels and the whirling emanations of a mirrored disco ball—? It's the turning point of each morning. And at its signal, I close the book that I've been reading since dawn and stare up at the lightplay for a quarter of an hour—before getting on with the other more concrete business of the day. I linger longer than usual this morning after discovering that I can alter the rhythm of the dazzle above me by throwing sacrificial portions of my breakfast eggs into the illuminated precincts of the pond. The subsequent agitation of that brilliant water—amplified by the feeding frenzy of the goldfish just beneath the surface— is translated immediately into an agitation of reflected light overhead. With my hardboiled egg hurling hands still raised in the air, I am the conductor of a luminous orchestra of luminous instruments.

A SHEPHERD'S TALE

29 March, 1997—Petulu, Bali—

for Wayan Subawa

You're sitting in a chair across from me on my porch. I've just finished eating my dinner and you've arrived for our usual nighttime *cerita cerita*—our after-dusk story *telling telling* hour. We'd already talked for a long time earlier in the afternoon—gossiping about the unfortunate German woman who built a house on the land opposite this porch and has been carrying on a tortured affair with a Balinese boy less than half her age—a 'playboy' who has, behind her back, been bedding dozens of the tourist girls who arrive here, as well as beating his all but abandoned Balinese wife whenever she complains about his behavior. Yet the tenor of the talk has changed with the cozy descent of darkness. This is no longer a voice tuned to village gossip, but the voice of village elegy. Eyes lowered, you mumble, *"I have a memory now . . ."* And then there is a long pause, longer than usual. I wait, contentedly serenaded by crickets, until you begin to relate the tale of the boy you'd once been: an eleven or twelve-year-old boy acting as his family's proud duck shepherd. My ears grow instantly bottomless. On this porch, in this hot equatorial night, I recall quite suddenly taking that short-cut home from the beach in Portugal, blazing a trail through hundreds of belled sheep—all of them watched over by a single old man in a heavy ragged vest who stared at me as I passed with no expression on his sun-browned face other than a leathery lifelong squint. *Seribu bebek,* you insist, *one thousand ducks.* And you hold to this figure despite my playful skepticism. "That's not *so* many," you persist. And after all, I think, what in the whole wide world do I really know about it anyway? You'd have to sleep out all night in the *sawah*, in a *pondok*, a rudimentary little shelter made of palm leaf and bamboo and maybe a sheet or two of corrugated tin or all-purpose blue plastic. Early in the morning when you woke, you'd gather up any fresh duck eggs

135

and take them in to the market in town to sell—leaving the ducks to fend for themselves until afternoon.

That toothless old man with wire arms that I watch crouched down beside the road all day with his rusty scythe—was he once as young as this boy you have become tonight, hurrying to the rice fields after school, cutting and hauling the long grass for your father's two cows, racing the darkness home? No wonder you were unable to endure more than a few months of that first paying job, those 12-hour shifts cooped up in that hot and greasy mechanic's garage. No wonder you quit so soon—spoiled by memories of long cool silent dawns filled with bamboo baskets heavy with ducks' eggs. I have a memory now too—of an innocence *not* my own, of the loss of an innocence I myself have *never* known. A memory of your eyes shining through the darkness, the eyes of a barefoot boy. And pyramids of eggs in the noisy marketplace. And the long-lost youth of men and nations.

OLD CORN

30 March, 1997—Petulu, Bali—

All my little snacks are gone—no peanuts, no dried banana chips, no crackers, no fruit—so I open a can of corn and eat the whole thing with salt and pepper. Never mind that it was originally canned by Del Monte, according to the faded green label, in 1989. Eight years ago, and still tender and bright yellow! I'm sure Indonesian grocery stores are casually filled with such tin-canned miracles of antiquity. The body really is rather easily fueled when the appetites of mind are busy elsewhere.

NET PROFIT

Even a life full of holes,
a life of nothing but waiting,
is better than no life at all.
      —Driss Ben Hamed Charhadi

              31 March, 1997—Petulu, Bali—

A late afternoon cloud slips slowly over the baked blue of the sky. And all the brilliant ladders of light cast onto bedsheets through palm fronds and half-shuttered windows have vanished in one moment, they've melted and ceased climbing. Another moment, and the cloud will pass. The ladders of light will return. But this time perhaps with a bit of breeze as well, shaking the palms, tearing the glowing pattern they paint—till this more ragged rise and fall, as of shredded fishnets, hauls in its weightless catch of bright nothing once again. So another afternoon leaks silently through tattered threads, leaving little behind but time, time to sleep beneath a sky filled with pin-pricks of stars—which leak light as well, yet a light more distant, a veteran light, a light already conversant with the end not of one day, but of all days.

It's *'a life full of holes'* as the Moroccan storyteller puts it, full of exquisite emptiness, lighter and lighter—that lone adjective *exquisite* being the very last thing it can hold—the life net's ultimate cargo, the last of the luminous to drain away through the loosened weave.

ROOM #35 RE-VISITED

1 April, 1997—Kuta, Bali—

Everything seems the same here—except for the towels which have changed from ten-year-old brown to brand-new white; and the curtains whose white vines on a blue field have become blue vines on a white field; and the little complimentary plastic bottle of shampoo in the basket in the bathroom which is still green but now smells more like oregano than spearmint; and the price, two dollars more per night; and last but not least my reflection in the bathroom mirror, emerging through condensing shower steam, washed clean of all but the passing years. On second thought—little remains the same considering how little has changed.

PRINTS

2 April, 1997—Kuta, Bali—

Sitting on the porch, drinking hot unsweetened black tea, I notice several footprints on the clean white tiles—very faint, but definitely human. My brow furrows momentarily, my sense of privacy alerted, if not alarmed. Then I recall that the tea I am drinking is delivered just before dawn each morning by a sleepy boy who slips his sandals off on the bottom step before crossing the porch tiles. Despite the hum of the ceiling fan, I usually hear him when he deposits the thermos and a small bunch of bananas on the wooden table outside my door. I like to rise before dawn, when it's still dark, and the arrival of the tea and bananas is a gentle signal to roll out of bed. This morning it was raining, there was mud in the garden, and perhaps the boy forgot his sandals entirely. This evening, on closer inspection, I notice the tiniest of insects, dozens of them, gathered around one of those footprints, nibbling at its muddy perimeter.

TROPICAL BREUGHEL

3 April, 1997—Poppies Lane, Kuta, Bali—

They are repairing the road here, without closing it to traffic. In the shifting thirty-yard stretch where work is most intensely focused there is a brutal and yet casually comical intensity of detail crammed into every available corner of space. A truck, belching hot smoke, dumps load after load of chalky stones, littering the landscape with little flesh-colored mounds. Women, their heads and faces wrapped in rags, mummified against dust and harsh sun, scoop them up, one shallow pan at a time. They pass these heavy pans to other women who carry them on their heads—and who hand them off, in a continuous relay, to still others who then scatter the pale pink stones over the raw roadbed. A band of young men follows close on their heels. Armed with sledgehammers, they smash the layers of stone, while others stand by to rake them evenly only moments before a prehistoric steamroller completes the job with a deafening roar, crushing and flattening. The steamroller is, of course, more than half the width of the entire route, as are the mini-vans loaded with the luggage of those checking in or out of the small budget hotels that line this roadway-in-renovation. In the meantime, the temporary eye of each and every ever-shifting needle of space is threaded by yet another darting motorbike swerving to avoid one of the hundreds of sunburned, near-naked tourists who interrupt the roadwork, not simply by the logistical fact of their passage, but due to the brazen dead-stopped stares of the army of fully clothed sledgehammer bearers, as well as the countless adolescent would-be entrepreneurs who surround those trapped in traffic to hawk their baskets of beach-towels and sarongs, their racks of hats and sunglasses, their boxes of knock-off watches and cheap perfumes. No surprise that, in all this din, a stray dog, plagued with mange, seems deaf to the honking horn of the vehicle in front of which it has collapsed in the very hub of high noon's heat to scratch the last remaining tuft of hair from its hide.

If you are in no hurry, it is a master class in composition. But if you are convinced that there is some place that you must be, something that you must do, if there is nothing running through your mind but your own long since completed superhighway, then you shut your eyes tight or grind your teeth, you sigh, or you mutter. Or, as in the case of one blindly determined motorcyclist, one red-faced and sweating piece of the puzzle, you curse the island's mischievous gods aloud.

GOING NOWHERE

10 April, 1997—Petulu, Bali—

Once again it's *Hari Raya Nyepi*, the Balinese New Year—a day of silence and a night of darkness—no traffic on the roads, no traveling *out*, no work, no lights, all this so that any evil spirits passing over the island will be deceived into believing that there is no mischief to be made here and so move on to other less ritually fortunate locales. Last night, more drastic measures were taken. At about eight o'clock, just past dark, five men and one wide-eyed boy entered the garden, banging pots and cans with cutlery, and wielding fragrant burning brooms with which they alternately beat and swept the ground in an effort to drive out any stray demons by fear and force—at the same time censing the evening air with thick, sweet smoke. What a lovely emptiness I felt as I sat silent in the dark after they'd moved on, the lingering incense perfuming the cloth of my shirt and mingling with the mist rising around the edges of the fishpond alongside my purged porch.

And now, all day today—a peace that is like a megaphone for birds and frogs and wind in the leaves and cicadas in the trees and falling drops of rain from thatched eaves and several distant deafening collapsing corridors of silver-plated thunder. It is machines that are responsible for most of the music of modern life, and when each and every one of them, from the radio and the television to the blender and the air-conditioner, is abruptly switched *off*—then one can hear a more primal murmur—. One can hear earthworms rolling over underground in the mud where coal is born with a low sigh. One can hear the roots of trees chattering in the buried echo chambers where diamonds begin their infinite opera of humming mirrors. When each and every car engine stops, one can hear from half a mile away (without having to drive there) the beating of the wings of a single bird, a startling sound. Even the giant spider webs strung up between banana palms will sing, when gilded by sunlight, like the nervous systems of harps. But only, of course, after men and women turn off all their kitchen appliances, all beaters and juicers, and slicers and graters and tick-tocking timers, and plunk themselves down in their creaking chairs to listen to their hair grow and gray and then fall out. Ants carry the fallen hairs away almost immediately, tap-dancing in a long parade to the music of rapid eye-blinks—.

Today I am going nowhere.

GARDEN RAMPANT

13 April, 1997—Petulu, Bali—

The shaft of sunlight is empty, then it is suddenly filled with thousands of tiny red round specks descending slowly through the air, an atomic shower—of seeds, I soon surmise. Somewhere overhead a pod must have burst, or the dead and dried heart of a flower finally succumbed to rot and dispersal and released its last will and testament—which would have remained invisible to me were it not for a certain angle formed by my eye and the light, an angle called illumination. The air here, in this garden rampant, must be filled with that sort of fertility all the time—a perpetual motion that never ceases even when wind drops or light fails to reveal. How many of those seeds, coursing through the air, landed on my toast this morning even as I lifted it to my mouth? And what strange fruits are already being prepared within me by all the other seeds and soils of which I am continually composed and decomposed.

145

SPIDER WRITER

18 April, 1997—Petulu Bali—

How do you begin—? That central snowflake of spittle is remarkable enough in design—but how, speck of a creature, do you manage to hang that highwire two thousand times your own length on which to perform your act of spin? Do you just let loose long sticky threads and wait for any wind to anchor them to any leaf or twig in the garden, casting blind fortune's bridges over gaps and chasms of space? Once begun, do you delight in opportunities grown as complex as the weave itself? Does your web seem infinite? And how long must you then sit there, trapped, all but woven into your own design—until that same wind which guided you once, shifts direction, tatters all your silk, and turns and tears the pages of your book left out in the garden overnight?

WAITING, WATCHING

24 April, 1997—Petulu, Bali—

Four or five weeks here—and the presence of stillness, or the absence of habitual activity, is translated into a heightened sensitivity to detail. For the first week or so of lovely coma this was expressed more in hallucination: like when I was sitting on the porch after dark in a downpour, and the moonlight reflecting off the wet leaves in the garden suggested all sorts of things to my hyper-awakened eye—everything from a ballerina twirling around a slender rain-slick stalk of bamboo—to a dwarf in a sombrero playing an accordion of fern—to a crocodile with its dark green snout shoved on backwards. Yet these illusions were but a prelude, an initiation. For now the things I see are more often quite real, and really there—and there—and there—. Like the praying mantis I spotted this morning from all the way across the pond. Or those two frogs, one sleeping atop the other, on a branch near the old stone wall that keeps my bathroom from dropping off the cliff into the river gorge below. Then there are the more obvious materializations, traveler's gold, lucky gifts of random times and places. Like the two goldfish salesmen I pass by chance one hot afternoon, sprawled out in the shade of the awning of a closed store, sound asleep—while beside them, wide awake, in clear plastic bags clustered like transparent grapes at either end of the long bamboo pole used to carry them, dozens of golden fish circle round and round, eyes wide, almost as wide as mine, waiting, watching, waiting, watching, waiting, watching.

BEARING PERFUMES

A long day of idle travel today on the back of Wayan's motorbike. With no need to steer, I found my eyes closing from time to time, lids lowered against the glare of sun and the rush of wind, delighted by the succession of smells as we went speeding through the changes in the landscape—up into the mountains to the edge of the lake, through countless roadside villages, then down again from cool groves of snake-apple and mangosteen to long hot stretches of terraced rice field, and finally through the narrow crumbling mudbrick alleys of his childhood home in Mengwi—where we stopped for a cracker and a warm cola with his family before returning down a potholed road lined with the ramshackle shops of masons and carvers, trailing scents of sandstone dust and chips of hibiscus wood all the way home to my porch—where I am packing now for my departure tomorrow morning for the coast.

It's through the intimacy of fragrance that I have really begun to know this place, through the cloves burning in tobacco, through the ubiquitous stench of morning and evening trash fires, of frying coconut oil and freshly scythed grass, through the sickly-sweet incense of overripe bananas, through the dull rot of *sawah* mud baking in noonday sun, and through the sudden rain which has a different odor for every overheated surface it cools with its touch, from leaf to stone to skin. Even that after-sun lotion I've just packed alongside my towel and my sandals, the one I used as lubricant when Mamat fucked me what seems like a thousand years ago in the scrub of stunted palms that bordered the stretch of shoreline we would hike to each morning. I zip up my travel bag, lay out my travel clothes, but still the coming week that I will spend at the beach seems imaginary—as the moments always do until they arrive, bearing perfumes.

148

TRAVELER'S QUESTION

5 May, 1997—Kuta, Bali—

I've put this journal away, packed it securely in my bag, and am slipping into shoes and socks for only the second time in two months, preparing to just sit and wait for the remaining half hour until my transport arrives to take me to the airport—when I spy some sort of centipede-like creature crawling, with a million tiny legs feverishly wriggling, across the white tiles of my porch. *Traveling,* I think to myself, *now that's traveling.* The insect is moving in a perfectly straight line until I tap it ever so slightly with one tentative fingertip. Immediately it buckles in the middle, then curls round from one end, tucking in its head defensively—its entire body transformed into the top portion of a suddenly stationary question mark. I sit back down on my chair, staring at my punctuated porch tiles, waiting, as this minor query gradually uncurls, hesitates, reorients itself—and then continues on—straight as a slow-motion arrow, in that direction I am not convinced it is aware that it has been traveling all along.

(FOUR AND A HALF MONTHS LATER)

CONVICT

Increasingly overgrown, the garden around the porch of this neglected back bungalow seems to be reaching a point beyond manicure. Now that the pond has been filled in—its reflections of the sky lost, like a last way out—I feel, while sensing the sun trying to rise over the rim of a bank of rainclouds barely visible through gaps the breeze opens in the enclosing foliage, as if I am in a sort of cage. But a cage whose bars are all curled in embrace, a cage of palm fronds, laced up and interlocking at odd green angles, a cage whose walls are living sparks and snakes and fecund fireworks. Even the humble bouquet of welcome snipped from the jungle and potted on my little marble table on the day of my arrival, plays its part—its silhouette woven, in pre-dawn light, into the ragged hedge of hibiscus rising behind it. Yes, it's a ferociously delicate prison, this calm crisscrossing of silent swords of sap dripping with last night's rain, quivering like iron bars would if they could. Sitting here, sipping tea in half-light, I am indeed a happy convict—cradled rather than captured by the relentlessly tentative curves of earth and light.

MOVE MOVE MOVE

5 November, 1997—Petulu, Bali—

My eyes have been tuned at last and are actually capable of responding, from fifty paces, to the frantic industry of a convention of red ants on the trunk of the rambutan tree. They've been there all week, but suddenly I notice them, suddenly they cannot be ignored. Busy myself, with my laundry, in between rinsings I hurl buckets of water at them to give them something unforeseen to chatter about with their translucent orange antennae. Everything and everyone seems to be working hard this year. Time itself seems to be passing with a movement reminiscent of perspiration—each day of fresh toil rises to the surface of the skin like sweat, then cools and dries into evening and deep sleep.

I'm off to Kuta in a day—I have to clear out of here because the whole place is booked as some sort of package deal to a tour group from Taiwan. I know the new owner is praying that it will not rain, that the leaking roof thatch will remain his well-kept secret—his and mine. So I'll do a brief stint at the beach to revive my coastal instincts, shop for some silver, trip in some potholes, and marvel at the decay of culture ushered in by vacationing Westerners in 10-day increments of unrelenting leisure. Then I'll hurry back up here, into the mountains, to finish up my work, work, work. At some point a long afternoon will find me with nothing to do but watch the sweltering shadows on the wall beside my bed shift and sway with the failed promises of a hot breeze. And I'll pray for rain, of course—manna and mesmerizing music of the tropics. Until then I will have to content myself with this furious activity, with purpose, with forward motion.

And if the future proves too flimsy a substitute until the as-yet unattainable present moment materializes, I can always find refuge in the past. I can always inhabit reverie. I can always dream back, while I move move move forward. Just this morning, passing through Andong, I was thinking about B, thinking how lucky he was to have had those few idyllic pre-electrified years in his now vanished house in the wide-open rice fields. One afternoon, after a snack on his porch, when I reached for a broom to clean up the crumbs that littered the cracked tiles at our feet, I remember how he slowly waved his hand through the air to stop me, saying, "Don't bother. The ants will clean up after us. They never stop working." Oh, the house may still be there—renovated, enlarged, the warped rattan of its walls replaced with rigid cinderblocks, the thatched eaves now tiled or tinned, the plumbing re-routed indoors—but it can't be seen from the road, blocked as it is now by all the other houses that have sprouted up from the long since drained steps of the sawah. —Yet if I close my eyes.....

.....ahhhh, here's the breeze at last, blowing thought right out of the head, seducing the long folds of the mosquito net, percussioning the palms, and gently lifting the corners of this page in my journal as if to turn it. Even the wind conspires to ensure that yet another pleasant present moment passes out of reach.

NEXT TO A BLUE RUBBER BAND
AND A LIZARD'S TURD

6 November, 1997—Petulu, Bali—

Shopping, sweating, hauling, sweating, unpacking, sweating, re-packing, sweating, counting, sweating, sweating, stop—. What do I see—? My laundry steaming in the sunlit garden. The broken eggshells of my breakfast littering the marble tabletop. A few coarse grains of spilled salt on the porch tiles, next to a blue rubber band and a lizard's turd. A plastic bottle of soy sauce with a little magic ring of mold around the tip. Seven ripe mangosteens. A single kamboja blossom, fallen to the ground, its bright white petals darkening to deep lemon in the center where the sex is. A loom of light weaving on a crosshatch of coconut palms. My left foot glowing in a stripe of direct sun. A couple of passing clouds larger than I am.

FORGETTING FAUST

20 November, 1997—Tegallalang, Bali—

The village dogs alone take heed of my approach. One by one they relay the alarm, then follow barking on my heels—*get out of town!* They know full well that I do not belong. Yet territorial clamor soon exhausts itself once I emerge into the wide stepped green of terraced *sawah*. Here a calming silence reigns in sharp contrast to their hysteria. Here chance encounters with the same dogs find them mute, no foreign scent or step now drives them mad. Here nothing hinders the light passage of my ghost, returned to haunt this home it's never had. I've passed this way *so* many times—and still I feel the same romantic impulse, the same ache of awe, the same idealized and yet misplaced nostalgia for picture postcard landscapes spread before my starveling sense—a sense glutted by the crowded palette of modern life's supply, and its demands, yet come a beggar now to this serene green feast, this youthful idyll of more ancient man.

Sometimes I stop my steps completely—just to stand, to root myself, in reverie, to the land. And though I'd feel the first (or last) man on this earth, such selfishly heroic fantasies are soon belied by those small figures that I see crouched in the distance more immovably. A solitary form, remote, I soon move off—as if I'd no more meaning for *their* lives than some far jet-plane's noiseless arc which leaves the sky bright blue and empty once it's passed them by. A bit of alien weather, an unusual cloud, I linger for a moment. *They* remain—. And soon turn back, in silence, to their daily labor, crushed by the peace these fertile fields sustain.

To hymn a *"happy"* peasantry would be inane, I know, I know. And a rustic greeting card is far from my intention. Yet there's an emotion here I can't deny: a haunting aboriginal connection which our bold new technology has disallowed—a stable ground it's long since dis-established. Our furious machinery, by its own momentum, allied with longings in the human soul, has bred a most peculiarly rootless form of infinite desire: unsatisfied by even the most infinite of satisfactions it's doomed to artificially produce. The men we were, the rooted ones, *must* have possessed the same impulsive, wandering dreams of soul—but without complex means, without machines of transport to literalize each passing whim and fancy, such dreams bore but the vivid fruits of reverie: poor, naked, finite man's sole form of travel.

I see them here, out in these green, changeless fields—these men who have, somehow, been left behind. I see them seeking, at the hottest hour of day, some patch of shade in which they can recline and drift far from the scene of necessary labor, their trusted tools dropped mutely by their sides, the simplest breeze sufficient capital to launch them on some silent, magic carpet ride.

I can't just stop—. I can't just sit right down beside this road, can't vanish into these green fields. And so I merely turn around, retrace my steps, and pass once more through town—where barking dogs, those brutal heralds of arrival *and* departure, announce my flight into my future—borne upon the Boeing Mephistophelean Whirlwind that carries me to what I must call home.

WING SWEPT

20, November, 1997—Petulu, Bali—

They emerge right from the ground, in a certain season all their own, in huge self-destructing swarms. I was eating in a restaurant one evening, years ago, down near the river bank in Ubud, when bewildering clouds of them invaded the entire town, the frantic buzz and flutter of their outsized wings colliding with every available surface, every wall, every face, terrifying the uninitiated. Within less than a minute my soup bowl was filled to the brim—for this seasonal spasm of flight tears wing from body almost immediately, and the dismembered wings settle everywhere like small translucent leaves, abandoning their larval remainder to the whims of a host of eager predators. "*Dalu*" the Balinese call them, claiming that they were a good source of nutrition in days when meat was scarcer than it is today.

A quarter of an hour later the whole town was out sweeping, and the restaurant and the street outside were newly landscaped with tremulous mounds of these scarcely stilled wings. I still remember the strange sound those busy brooms made, a sort of crackling as of cellophane tearing in the distance. Unlike that first encounter, the next time I had fair warning and was instructed by the locals to turn off all the lights in my bungalow, so as not to attract them. Once the infestation had subsided, and the lights had been switched back on, I sat and watched as the wings that littered my porch came back to life again—the ants that hauled them away, one by one, all but invisible beneath their prized canopies. Tonight, on the eve of my departure, they have returned again, in even greater numbers. Out for a final walk in the garden in the dark, with my flashlight, I see that a herd of dancing faeries seems to have been fed to an invisible lawnmower. Everywhere the grass is carpeted with severed wings.

1998

THE WHOLE HARVEST

Gloucester:
No further sir. A man may rot even here.

William Shakespeare

THE ARRANGEMENT

15 July, 1998—Petulu, Bali

Squeezed out from a tube of metal into a bowl of green. And once more I play the part of the anxious astronaut, amazed all over again that there is indeed life on the other planet—caught unawares, yet again, by the crucial ritual of initiation which physical splashdown is only a pale shadow of. Yesterday I purchased a piece of furniture in a shop down the road: a dark wooden bureau, nearly as tall as myself, its eight drawers inlayed with mother-of-pearl. Well, one of these drawers didn't slide very smoothly and, fearing that it might be stuck fast by the time I received it in America, I suggested switching it with one of the other eight to see if perhaps a more practicable order might be arrived at. So, for the next several minutes, like an under-rehearsed vaudeville team, I and my friend and a bewildered but nonetheless co-operative shopkeeper unsystematically exchanged each and every drawer over and over again, trying to find the ideal arrangement. *"How about this one—? " "How about this one—?" "Maybe this one—?" "Or this one? —" "How about this one—?" "Which one—?" "This one—." "No, this one—!" "Did we try this one—?"* Until I took that crucial step backward, fell offstage, and just burst out laughing, shoving them all in any-old-which-way-possible. Ever since that moment of laughter an accumulated tension has been draining out of me—gushing out at first, giving me a headache in the process, but by now, a week into my journey, slowing to a drip-drop-drip, to a tick-tock-tick, leaving me delightfully limp, passive, receptive to any arrangement of life's drawers.

BLINDNESS

25 July, 1998—Petulu, Bali—

I remember when they were plural, when there were billions of them here—nighttime was a confusion of near and far, still and moving stars. Apparently they have fled the shifting frontiers of civilization, for I haven't seen a firefly in years. Tonight it seems their final ambassador is breathing and blinking his last. It can't fly any longer so I deposit it gently on the porch table where it spirals around amongst books and cups and saucers—a damaged sports car with one green tail lamp, or a tiny robot running amok and backwards, blinded in its one mechanical eye. I've always been partial to characters who lose their eyes in tragedy—either one, or the other, or both. Would it be going too far, as it approaches my dog-eared paperback Shakespeare, to christen this poor dying ember Gloucester?—whose fate has always seemed to me far harsher than his king's, for madness can protect a dramatic insect from things not even blindness can erase. *"The king is mad. How stiff is my vile sense that I stand up and have ingenious feeling of my huge sorrows! Better I were distract; so should my thoughts be severed from my griefs, and woes by wrong imaginations lose the knowledge of themselves."* The curtain of darkness falls at last on my copy of Lear—the final firefly not yet dead, but nevertheless extinguished on its cover. As I rave on.

MY KINGDOM FOR A BREEZE

26 July, 1998—Petulu, Bali—

"A breeze! A breeze! My kingdom for a breeze!" cried a very wealthy king on a very hot and sultry evening. And so powerful a king was he that his wish was instantly granted—. His kingdom and all it contained vanished in the blink of one eye, wafted away, and he found himself sitting, not under the gilded canopies of its gardens, but in the middle of a wide and empty plain, beneath a single flowering tree. In the distance he could make out the lights of a palace, perhaps his own—but as he watched, those lights flickered out one by one and he was left all alone. As if from out of nowhere then, a cool and fragrant breeze arose, laving his skin, rustling his hair.

300 PAPER BUGS

3 August, 1998—Kuta, Bali—

In years past, I'd eyed those primitively painted paper bugs for
sale on any street corner here in Kuta, always amused by the
straightforward physics of the spool-and-thread mechanism
hidden in their bellies—a simple machine, a kind of yo-yo
which, when pulled by an elastic string threaded through the
cardboard carapace, causes them to scurry across the ground.
And all without batteries! Ingenious toys! I was convinced they'd
be a great item to import to the States for low-budget impulse
sales in my store, but had always been too timid to engage the
somewhat shady Javanese street vendors who cobbled them
together from cast-off materials and then set up open-air shops
at dusk in heavily touristed intersections. This evening, with
uncharacteristic confidence, I overwhelm one peddler with
dreams of grandeur by asking him how much he would charge
for 300 pieces. He immediately springs into action, grasping
at opportunity with a natural aggression that puts my years
of reticence to shame. I end up sputtering all over town with
Hari on the back of his motorbike as he rounds up the requisite
number of handmade cockroaches and beetles and ants and
spiders and even a dozen or so 'special' lobsters with paper claws.
Two hours later, I am collapsed on my porch alongside two black
plastic trash bags bulging with herds of insects at fifty cents a
head. What now?—I think. What mountain shall I scale next?

THE BEARD

4 August, 1998—Petulu, Bali—

Wayan tells me today that the Balinese have a saying: *'a man's money is like his beard'*—, it grows and then it's shaved off, it grows back and then is shaved again, and again, again, again. I am surprised at first by this attitude towards the inevitability of both wealth *and* poverty. Given the often-humble circumstances of village life here, I should have expected only the latter to have figured prominently in the proverbial play. Like most city dwellers, I underestimate the rural rhythms of the whole harvest.

1999

IT'S ALL GOING

The road climbed steadily. It was hard work walking up-hill.
His muscles ached and the day was hot, but Nick felt happy.
He felt like he had left everything behind, the need for thinking,
the need to write, other needs.
It was all back of him.

Ernest Hemingway

One must need to go there.

Belden C. Lane

STATIONS OF THE CROSSING

22 February, 1999—Petulu, Bali—

Before his myth of himself walked off into the Ohio snow, away from his business and his family, Sherwood Anderson left the following note: *"There is a bridge over a river with cross-ties before it. When I come to that I'll be alright. I'll write all day in the sun and the wind will blow through my hair."* A bit hyperbolic perhaps, but that's just what we ask of a good nervous collapse. There's pouring rain tonight here at my own crossing, there's a continual dripping from thatch and from garden leaf, and one lone frog carrying a rather irregular bass-line. What about these crossings—? Aren't they where blues guitarists were supposed to make deals with the devils of their art, there where X marks the spot? And where those fabulous phallic stones were erected to Hermes? They're obviously great outdoor cruising sites, veritable temples of choice. Thrilling, but alas only a brief respite from the long and winding road that snakes uphill and down like a howl rising and falling in wind. So cover my eyes, spin me round three times, and I'll be on my own way.

SPIDER'S HOUSE

23 February, 1999—Petulu, Bali—

It all stems from my inability to move today. It all starts with my irresistible temptation to throw things into the enormous spider webs festooning the garden. The spiders are about four inches across, maybe more. Fruit peels, grass, twigs, leaves, cracker crumbs—all come in handy. I'm a mischievous boy with a slingshot.

In gradually growing reverie, I am another little boy, a fictional boy, who steals his young sister's dollhouse furniture and throws that into another web, a fictional web, the web of the story. The little chairs and tables and sofas remain suspended there, stuck fast in mid-air, while a larger and larger spider creeps over to investigate. What the story does not reveal is how the web grows so enormous that, later, even life-sized chairs and sofas and tables hang from its sticky threads, drained of their accustomed weight.

PETTY AS A PICTURE POSTCARD

25 February, 1999—Petulu, Bali—

There's green and gray today and not much else. No work, not much talk, just books, just thought, just leaves as big as or even bigger than my head, just this low ceiling of quiet cloud over the quiet garden—threatening, or promising. There *was* one brief downpour earlier, each fat drop distinctly audible as it hit the ground—but the squall soon passed, and the not-much-else returned. Wayan just puttered off reluctantly on his motorbike, headed to his village to hash out some family crisis—it's that greedy uncle again, the one who keeps claiming all the communally inherited land of a recently deceased patriarch, trying to sell it off to buy cars and appliances and other things of little or no use to him or anyone else in the rice fields. Ah yes, the pettier the problem, the more annoying it can become. Of course, I left all my own petty problems behind when the airplane hatch closed with that soft sucking sound and the overhead compartments clicked shut—. So I can just sit here on my porch on a gray and green day and take the oh-so-relaxed higher ground—. Nevertheless, I do from time to time regale Wayan with picaresque tales of my own petty life back home, and we sit chortling as dusk falls gently around the edges of the truth that what's petty *there* is petty *here,* and vice-versa. But no more tales today. Just gray. Just green.

DANGLING IN THE WATER

26 February, 1999—Petulu, Bali—

Sitting with my feet dangling in the abandoned swimming pool, examining all the little leaves and drowned insects floating on the surface, I spy what appears to be a tiny piece of jewelry or a sparkling button—and I scoop it out—only to have it sprout sudden legs and cling to my finger when I try to deposit it on wet blue tiles. It *is* an insect, but it looks like a gem—its wings drenched almost to transparency, yet crossed with faint golden hieroglyphs that catch fire in the sun. For a few moments it crawls about, opening and closing its wings in order to dry them. Then it vanishes, like a lost golden earring longing to regain its anonymity. I turn my attention back to the water, this time rescuing a tiny spider that has sought refuge on a raft of three fortuitously converging mango leaves. A moment later an orchid trailing a lace of green tentacles slips from the mossy groin of an otherwise barren branch of frangipani, and plummets to the ground. An old woman arrives then, to lay her daily offering at the threshold of the tiny temple nearby—followed ever so quickly and quietly by a cat who scales the stone steps of the shrine to gobble up the sacred grains of boiled rice from the very lap of God. All this I observe light-headedly in the glaring sun, dripping sweat, before the afternoon thunderclouds already massing in the north begin to roll in, and the wind begins to rise. It isn't until I get back to my room that I realize that my key is lost, that it must have fallen from the pocket of my shorts while I was swimming in the deep end of the deserted pool.

EMPTIED EYES

27 February, 1999—Petulu, Bali—

He's been resting right on top of her all throughout this stormy afternoon, from time to time bewildering one of her dry, tired teats. Not that she seems to mind. She just lies there motionless, except for her empty green eyes, pale as seawater in fog, which follow every little move I make. As the storm was approaching this morning, they were sleeping soundly on the little concrete steps at the base of my bungalow, awakened only when the eaves above them began to drip and splatter. I opened up my black umbrella and wedged it between the steps and the side of the house, but its shelter didn't prove particularly inviting. After lying inside on my bed reading for an hour or more, scribbling in this journal and on a few postcards curling up around their humid edges, I went out to sweep the water off the flooded porch—and peeking around the corner of the house I saw that both of the cats, undernourished mother and overgrown child, had at last deigned to take refuge beneath my umbrella. The storm shows no signs of letting up, and I'll sit watching them for hours—my otherwise emptied eyes following every little move they make.

TO MY PUBLISHER

28 February, 1999—Petulu, Bali—

I dream that I am dying last night. It's terrifyingly funny (at least in retrospect) due to the fact that my doctor is none other than JM, my publisher—and due to the fact that he has a habit of disappearing, of wandering away at crucial medical moments. The initial crisis stems from my inability to breath, and it is he who calms me and places the oxygen mask firmly on my face. The problem is in my left lung, he explains as he leads me through a series of white swinging doors—gently guiding me with soothing tones through the details of my life-threatening condition. The odd thing is—he will suddenly walk away, sometimes in mid-sentence, distracted by some equally pressing concern—and I will be left there, stranded, with the seed of death lodged in my chest. Once, while following about twenty paces behind him, I watch helplessly as he simply vanishes around a corner. I soon find myself on the threshold of some inner sanctum of sickness which I am forced to reconnoiter on my own, ostensibly in search of either doctor or publisher. I do locate him at last, unflappable as always, but only after stumbling through two library-like rooms lined with row upon row of beds in which the terminally ill lay in a meticulously choreographed catalogue of sickness, their limbs the letters of an alphabet of calm suffering. I think, when I finally catch up with him, he says something like—*"Oh, there you are!"*—and laughs lightly.

INNER BABOON

2 March, 1999—Petulu, Bali—

Spiders with orange stripes on their long and crooked legs, mosquitoes and darting bats at dusk, enormous lizard turds on the porch tiles at dawn, violent weather, and these chronic ant caravans crossing my own less persistent path—. How much simpler *they* are to deal with than erratic taxi-cab drivers, overdue utility bills, and the cell-phone ring-tones of weekend bar-hoppers. I'm seriously thinking of switching species and have been researching baboons on the desert plateaus of Ethiopia— you know—the ones with those huge bald red butts that so embarrass the bourgeoisie at zoos. They like to sit on high dry cliffs to watch the sunrise and the sunset. I think I might be able to find a perch there. I think I could call them brothers.

JUNGLE JUNG

4 March, 1999—Petulu, Bali—

Tourists trying to share a Javanese whore in the bungalow next to mine raised quite a ruckus last night. Sitting in silence and in darkness, I was startled from reverie—my cool porch tiles suddenly scorched by the beam of a hand-held torch erupting on surfaces near and far in the pitch-black garden. Searching treetops and rooftops, bushes and garden paths, someone was stamping through the flowerbeds, barking imprecations, apparently on the scent of something *awful*. After a while I called out for bit of quiet—not even bothering to ask what it was all about—and a couple of voices in the dark half-heartedly apologized. Retiring as the commotion began to subside, I lay watching the torchlight still splashing about on my bedroom walls for another half hour or so. This morning Wayan explains that the two men claimed to have seen someone peering in through their window from the dark garden. Of course, one can't help but wonder what they were doing in there to make them so paranoid. I am quite taken aback by the worldliness of my village friend's simple and candid theory: one of the two was having sex with the hired woman, while the other was spying on the scene from outside—and was then forced to chase his own guilty shadow around the garden, covering his own tracks. The woman, I imagine, just sat smoking while the two men danced around together outside—rolling her eyes with the patience of the numb—already counting the handful of small change she'd not yet been paid.

DEAD AND BROKEN

7 March, 1999—Batubulan, Bali—

On the way we pass a man and his young sons splashing around in the roadside gutter, disemboweling a huge hog that lies on its back, four feet poking at the sun, gut slit to the sky. The father is reaching in to remove long strings and gobs of viscera, depositing them in a steaming heap which his children gather round laughing. The pig is far larger than any of his sons. That's all I see, for the whole scene is left behind in an instant by the speeding motor beneath us and the road that slips constantly away. Not long afterward the traffic slows to a standstill—an accident, of course. As we cautiously approach, Wayan stiffens. "*Mati,*" he whispers hoarsely in my ear, "*Dead.*" As he steers the motorbike into a patch of weeds at the side of the road, we see that a crowd has gathered around the body of what seems no more than a boy. They are covering his face with a white cloth and rolling him up into a stained bamboo mat. Wayan asks me for a few *rupiah*, then instructs me to wait for a moment while he strides through the crowd to add them to the pile of coins that already lies beside the crudely mummified body. As he moves forward, offering in hand, two small boys run backward from the corpse, playfully, as from a wave on the shore of death. Pausing alongside me, the elder of the two pantomimes the split head and smashed nose of the victim, both boys giggling gruesomely as they scamper off a moment later. On our way once again, driving very slowly now—for the Balinese always drive very slowly for at least a *few* moments after witnessing an accident— Wayan casts a worried glance over his shoulder which I can't help but misinterpret. "*Sedih?*" I ask him, gently, "*Sad?*" "Flat," is his only reply as he pulls over yet again and dismounts to inspect our rear tire, punctured perhaps by a piece of the broken glass that littered the scene of the accident. The noon sun makes the walk seem longer, but it really only takes about fifteen or twenty

179

minutes to reach the *bengkel* in the nearest village where we have the tube replaced for 18,000 *rupiah*. Eyeing the sweat rolling down my brow, the mechanic throws in a couple of cold drinks for free, for pity's sake.

FOR A FADING CITY OF SOUL

7 March, 1999—Kuta, Bali—

The latest *development* here—? The grand opening of a blaring cassette shop in the alley alongside my bedroom wall where the last remaining row of old *warungs* has at last been torn down. It's *all* going, all the shabby old-world charm, all replaced by spic-and-span public restroom architecture spiced with cloying surf-centric motifs. Even the half-assed little bookstore where I used to buy my out-of-date newspapers has vanished—the entire block razed to make way for yet another high concept mini-mall offering more-and-more-of-the-same for sale. The once ragged beachfront itself has been cut and hemmed, its spanking new centerpiece a three-story Hard Rock Café with Megastore downstairs—all corporate all singing all dancing—all sucked down with a complementary plastic straw. Nevertheless, the Balinese continue to place their offerings at the edge of the sea—whether reverently or only dutifully I am neither able nor willing to determine. Walking along the shoreline to breakfast this morning, I scan the evidence of last night's sacred bounty scattered by receding waves. The surfside sand is littered with purple petals, rotting bananas, young cracked coconuts, sealed plastic bags full of pale red tea, a single long green chili pepper swollen with salt water and split up the center. The gay morning-after confetti extends for miles, as far as the eye can see—a bright exhausted skyline for a fading city of soul.

THE DARK HALF

9 March, 1999—Kuta, Bali—

I swim for an hour beneath a sky half dark as death, half burning blue—then flinch, and flee at last for shelter, the dark half nipping at my heels all the way home. And though I feel always only one step ahead of the storm, it seems I have far outpaced it after all. I'm back in my room now, I've already showered all trace of sand and salt from my skin, and the only thing that has fallen from the sky are these unstable shadows. I settle down protected on my porch to face the threat of thunder in the distance, convinced that there'll be violence yet—.

2000

WITHIN RANGE
OF THE USUAL SUFFERING

I loaf and invite my soul.

Walt Whitman

GREEN BLUES

12 February, 2000—Campuan, Bali—

I catch sight of a row of insanely bright ragdolls hanging like puppets just inside the door of an empty shop on a deserted street. A woman sitting at the threshold, catching my caught eye, leaps to her feet and begins a feverish demonstration: lifting the absurd little skirts, unzipping the spines, extracting what seem at first no more than little parachutes of patchwork stuffing— but which turn out to be clever carrying purses in which to transport the dolls themselves once each ensemble has been turned entirely inside out. Still holding the eviscerated ragdolls, one in each hand, she announces that her husband died in a car accident two years ago. We both shake our heads from side to side in a gesture of sorrow as brief as our encounter, and then go on about our respective businesses—she hanging her once again lifeless puppets back up onto their hooks for perhaps the millionth time, me walking off down the road in the noonday sun in search of some ice-cold papaya juice with lime. It's hard to imagine singing the blues amidst so much green—but there's as much suffering in the garden as anywhere else, with the same chord progressions and the same aches and wonders. She'll need a name of course, some sort of tag with a catch—that is, if she wants her lament to echo down more than her own poor little street of poor little shops as she sings her abruptly matter-of-fact biography, her *Puppet Widow Blues*.

BEAST OR POET

13 February, 2000—Petulu, Bali—

The cat that has toppled the garbage bin overnight now passes silently by the porch without even looking up at me. Were I to make the slightest noise or movement she'd dart away instantly and vanish into the pre-dawn darkness of the garden, beyond the reach of my weak porchlight. But I write without a sound, and she glides likewise silently on by—. It is only at an hour like this one, all alone and a foreigner, before day breaks and cock crows, that I recover the perfect indolence that can make of man a beast or a poet.

TILL CHIN FIND REST ON BREAST

15 February, 2000—Petulu, Bali—

"I loaf and invite my soul," wrote Whitman, *"I lean and loaf at my ease and observe a spear of summer grass."* Possibly, probably, the head of a leaner and a loafer is far fuller of deed done than the life of many a man of unrelenting action. As usual my own head, as I sit on the porch, grows so heavy with phantasmal *heave-ho!* that it drags and dips from time to time till chin finds rest on breast. In the distance, above the sound of traffic running ceaselessly back and forth beyond my garden wall, I can hear the unloading of yet another truckload of heavy stones destined for yet another new building. One by one the stones tumble, cracking violently against each other as they're tossed down a hillside, heaping up in a ravine, hesitating there in stillness—but only for a moment—. Too soon they'll be shoved into yet another foundation for yet another temporary tower or tabernacle, another irresistible invitation to ruin.

DEMONSTRATION

16 February, 2000—Petulu, Bali—

The list of obstacles—oh, that's endless—always endless. But back here on my porch in Bali, I am promptly introduced to Wayan's six-month-old son whose eyes are so bright and beautiful that they could probably prevent car crashes and Alzheimer's disease and unnecessary forest fires if properly administered one deep gaze at a time. Not only that—this morning while in the shower, a spider demonstrated the reintegration of the rational with nature and the divisibility of the indivisible—all by weaving a round web in the sun streaming through a square skylight in the sloping ceiling.

There you have it—the hermetic ghost glowing at the center of all things—the circle squared in a child's eyes by a web in a window within range of the usual suffering.

NIGHTSHIFT

17 February, 2000—Petulu, Bali—

I wake up at 1:30 AM and read my watch upside down by torchlight. Thinking it close to six in the morning, I almost get up and brew coffee in the dark—though at the last moment my body refuses to believe in the nearness of dawn and hugs the bed like a bag of warm wet sand until I drift off to sleep again. So many more dreams waiting to come, to go. Yet unless I make a concerted effort, now, at recollection—all of the images they bring me will remain unharvested. There were fires and floods last night, and a missing object that had to be kept secret. I wonder what it was—. A handkerchief? A lit match? A sponge? A spelling error? A boat or a stolen banana or a cigar? I suppose I'll never know. All I know is that I wake up as if from a long day's labor—moving from a full dark day to a day full of light along a thin bridge of luminous pink and gray birdsong.

OF BRIDGES

19 February, 2000—Petulu, Bali—

I am not that anxious, I must confess, for news from home. Though the powerful temptations of this telecommunicative age so easily trump solitude, great distance remains for me the more fundamental force. Isn't it just such great isolating distances that create us as distinct individuals? And without them, where would we find the chasms for art and faith to navigate or for lovers to leap?

Now hold on a moment—!

How did a scarcely initiated rant against fax machine & computer inbox end up as a hymn to the circus of mad love's leaps? See? There it is again—that tremendous abyss, bubbling up even between sentences, gaping between the compelling points of one's own argument! I don't mind constellating, don't get me wrong, but to fill in *all* the vast spaces between stars can only cage heaven and make the thrilling speed of light unnecessary. Mightn't it be better, sometimes, to simply breathe the air—rather than shoot a signal through it? Respiration at least contracts *and* expands, in quiet balance. For ordering pizza, then—the electronic age. But for the sweet mystery of life—give me the ancient gap, crisscrossed by grand slow sailing ships, by rickety rope-and-plank footbridges, by the twinkle in the eye, the fire in the groin, and the word that sometimes slips from the very tip of the tongue.

DETOUR

It starts to rain and the gutters at the foot of the hill are clogged with trash as usual—so all the water rushing down the little street collects in the ravine, forming a lake which driver after driver has to decide whether or not to hazard crossing. Several powerful jeeps plough through with such impulsive speed that waves of water crest over hoods and windshields. The rain continues falling for over an hour, the lake growing larger—everyone sitting outside on their safely elevated stoops and stairs, cheering and jeering from beneath dripping eaves at each successful or unsuccessful passage. The inevitable crowd-pleasers are those miscalculating motorbikes which choke and then conk-out halfway across the lake. Wayan and I find ourselves laughing and hollering along with everyone else—our own motorbike parked just a few yards down the street, paralyzed until the rain subsides and the lake drains.

I don't seem to get much work done on an average day, and I have given up pushing too hard. There's always some interruption or other that eats up the time, whether it be a sudden downpour, clogged gutters, an unexpected encounter and interminable conversation, or a high price at the market which takes all afternoon to negotiate in half. Yesterday it was that queen of obstacles: a temple procession blocking the main road when we were on our way home from a restaurant in town. With dinner cooling in a plastic bag on my lap, I scanned the faces of each and every celebrant as they passed—from the square jaws of the butch and shirtless, to the shy smiles of the young and gilded, to the deeply etched lines of the old or the lowly. Each had to be given time enough, and space enough, to pass by. And at the silent center of their parade, borne in the arms of a priest all in white, was the offering for which perhaps the entire pathway had been ultimately cleared: a single young coconut sprouting one

191

aching green shoot from a crack in its side. After that, the rest was only gongs and bells and barefoot women wailing.

So, I surrender the efficiency of each day that it may bear unknown fruit. I'm home now, rain still trickling down contentedly after the latest deluge. I am convinced that it will be a cool night, a chilly morning, and that tomorrow I will no doubt accomplish a little something—just enough, and no more.

THEY TOO WILL HAVE FEVERS

22 February, 2000—Petulu, Bali—

Less than two weeks in—and already I've been infiltrated by whatever it is that worms its way into the intestines here in paradise. I should have been warned off by the cesspool of mud-slimed trash at the threshold of the village quack's office, but I went through the motions of pill & payment anyway. Today I will take the more direct approach. Over the years the local pharmacist's trial-and-error have proved a good gamble, and I've scribbled a list of symptoms & medications on the inside cover of this journal that may help to narrow the odds. I'll enter the shop unshowered, with a ton of wet bread in my head, with my teeth tartared and my gut treed by its own baying hounds. I'll take cool comfort in the white coat of the woman in attendance. I'll ante up, laying my coin down on the cracked glass counter as she humbly spins the wheel—while her children play outside, naked but for the dust they are sitting in. I can see them through the shop's backdoor, left ajar. They too will have fevers. She may know what to do.

A MOUTH ABOVE ME

24 February, 2000—Petulu, Bali—

Still sleepless, mind still yakking away, I stumble up against a particularly persistent hallucination. The wrinkles at the top of my sagging mosquito net have caught a stray ray of light streaming in through the window at the foot of my bed, a beam cast by the lamp burning on the porch of the bungalow next to mine. These illumined wrinkles are shivering in the wind from the ceiling fan I often forget to switch off before retiring. So light and wind become the supple shadows with which I am face to face all night long as I lie on my back in my bed until dawn—shadows flexible enough to conjure, quite convincingly, a mouth above me, a moving mouth whose lips are parted and shuddering, as if speaking. Suspended in the dark of nowhere, it is whispering urgently, just to me, all through the night. And there is no escaping it. I watch the lips move for an hour, forget about them for a while, and then look back only to find them still trembling in the dark. I even reach up and press one finger between them, and still the illusion is not shattered. Of course, I cannot catch a single word of what it is that they trying to tell me, but perhaps this is because I have neglected certain preliminary ablutions and devotions, because I have not yet made my *Ascent of Mount Carmel*, or gone for more than a few purifying nights without compulsively handling my own genitalia. Yet it *is* a privilege of sorts, one worthy of some hyper-sensitive Saint Hysteria, to have been given even this opportunity to fail to read its lips in the middle of a dark night of interminable tossing and turning.

GAP

1 March, 2000—Petulu, Bali—

There is a gardener here who's lost a front tooth in a recent motorbike accident. It is a very charged gap in an otherwise blank face. I've grown convinced that all his sweepings—fallen petals, crushed leaves, dead insects, splinters of bamboo, dusts, crumbs—all of it disappears through that gap in his front teeth. Sometimes he just stops, gripping the broken handle of his plastic bucket, and stands there and stares at me—not with his eyes so much as with that little vaguely malevolent doorway in his mouth which I fear might swallow *me* up as well were I to solicit even a slight smile by looking up from the book that I am reading.

THE MOWERS AND THE CLIPPERS

3 March, 2000—Petulu, Bali—

Clip, clip. The word doesn't look nearly as silly as it is beginning to sound. The young gardeners have been busy trimming the grass outside my window all morning, crouched down on their haunches, their knees up around their ears, their *clippers* chattering away like false teeth in a cartoon of the kind of cold they'll never know. How I loved operating those *clippers* when I was a child—we had a pair with handles of lemon-yellow plastic, and a spring action between the long blades that was a never ending source of amusement. The lawn was for an adult to '*mow*'—but the borders of paths and the cracks in sidewalks, those hard to reach places, they were for a child to '*clip*'—. There are no *mowers* here, these gardeners are more boys than men, and yet given the speed and persistence of their *clip clip clip* outside my window, the entire equatorial rain forest could be stripped and shaven before noon. It is indeed the meek who shall inherit the earth, and care for it ceaselessly.

YOUNG LOVE

4 March, 2000—Petulu, Bali—

As he gathered up last night's dinner dishes on his way back to the kitchen, I pointed out a pair of little white butterflies dancing over his shoulder. *"Pachar pachar,"* he remarked— which is the local euphemism for *darlings,* for sweethearts, for young lovers. Pausing at the garden gate, uncertain that I'd been able to translate, he turned and spat out each unexpectedly Shakespearian syllable like a piece of hard candy—*"RO-ME-OH-AND-JOO-LEE-ET"*—and then vanished around the corner with a wink and a smile and a comic clank of silverware.

The young lovers with their bright white wings are waltzing around *my* shoulders now, while over by the low stone wall beyond the pond another butterfly, this one yellow, is performing its own ritual of courtship around a blossom that resembles it in both size and hue—. Yet perhaps those are are not yellow wings at all. Perhaps they are only a pair of yellow petals that have been torn from the yellow flower, momentarily detained by an animating breeze before they fall to the ground or are swept off to some further precinct of the garden by a more passionate gust of wind.

NO AXE TO GRIND

5 March, 2000—Petulu, Bali—

I hear the loud crack, and I see the tree fall. The garden is empty of all arm and axe—and the tree, I am assured, has been felled from within by a particularly ravenous beetle whose frenzied black back legs are pointed out to me as it tries to extricate the rest of its body from a deep crevice in the now exposed wood. Nearby, wedged more calmly into an inner cavity, nests a pale larval bundle about four inches long, leaking a distressing brown nectar at the puncture point of an errant splinter. What if *'a tree falls in a forest'*—and no proverb is forthcoming?

ACROSS THE AQUA CERAMICS

7 March, 2000—Petulu, Bali—

From the corner of one eye, where it's captured within a droplet of sweat balanced on the tip of one drenched lash, I catch sight of the proverbial chicken crossing the road—but without the road. The noonday sun, demanding aching clarity from each and every line and color, treats the too-blue pool tiles with no mercy. They do not belong here in a landscape of terraced rice fields and village brick-and-tan. And now, in blinding silhouette, this white chicken comes high-stepping across the aqua ceramics, its crimson wattle dangling like a crushed strawberry, more Magritte than Magritte in this hallucinatory heat. The blink of an eye dislodges the drop of sweat. As I raise my head I expect to hear the squawk of a hen in flustered flight—yet she just stands there, as sun-addled as I, with all the dumb persistence of a drunk's new tattoo on the morning after.

FOR *RENÉ*

8 March, 2000—Petulu, Bali—

Although my smoothly tiled porch is considerably less dramatic than the slopes of Etna on which Chateaubriand's René is perched in perpetual romantic anguish—nevertheless I recognize the view.

> *"A young man full of passion,*
> *sitting at the mouth of a volcano and weeping*
> *over mortal men whose dwellings*
> *he can barely distinguish far off below him—"*

Mount Agung is quiet this morning, almost stealthy as it emerges from a bank of lavender cloud and a shadowplay of palm. I am far from its fires which have been quiescent for some years now. Nor am I *young*. And if it is true that I am *passion-filled*, such ardors seem to have been at least temporarily eclipsed. My heart is nowhere near my sleeve, my dick is in my pants, my eyes are dry—and my skull is on my shoulders, not in my hand. Such incongruent details need to be dispensed with summarily if am to recalibrate the moment. On the other hand, it can't be denied that I am far from the *dwellings of mortal men.* I haven't spoken with a soul in days.

Think of it this way. Fellow travelers, this René and I—yet total strangers—we pass one another on a road somewhere between Natchez and Singapore. And that brief moment of tangency proves sufficient for the transfusion of certain images. That is to say, we indulge in a moment of personal collage—which proves, once all is said and then said again, far larger than ourselves. On these squares of paper, these pages we carry so many of, we sketch our maps under the sign of the Alembic, adding the mysterious symbols and colors—*Gunung Agung, Etna, Petulu,* even *Pompeii* if we like, even *Camelot* or *Roanoke*—with a smudge of gray

200

pastel for distance and dwelling, with blue for the heights, and with gold in the depths. And then we tear our paper squares to bits, we let the pieces catch the breeze, and we vow to meet again someday, elsewhere.

> *"Throughout my life, I have had before my eyes*
> *an immense creation which I could barely discern,*
> *while a chasm yawned at my side."*

That bottomless furnace has never seemed closer than it does tonight, when the violence of the thunder startles me awake— and in the darkness the world recedes further and further, as the booming voice of the storm shudders through me with true intimacy.

PATTERN

9 March, 2000—Petulu, Bali—

At dusk, the frangipani tree is essentialized—it turns to ink and rice paper right before my eyes as the light retreats from foreground to background, silhouetting its naked branches against what remains of the sky. Then at dawn, after a night of heavy rain, with consummate temporal symmetry the tree reappears, reversed now, reflected in a large puddle on my porch. This time it's joined by the reflection of a damp copy of the *International Herald Tribune*—dated Wednesday, March 8, 2000—yesterday's news draped over a wooden clothes dryer resting alongside this pool of cinema. Reflected in such an ascetic mirror the words of the newspaper disappear—the book of current events becomes a blank slate—. Likewise all color and texture are drained from the branches of the tree which drip downward now rather than rise up. It's a lovely if somewhat somber pattern, printed on a piece of fabric too slight to serve as anything more than a veil between passing moments.

NO DAWN

12 March, 2000—Petulu, Bali—

There were some mighty confused cocks this morning when thunder clapped—when clouds quickly smothered the sun, and heavy rain extinguished it once and for all, without so much as a hot hiss, in cold water. There was no dawn today. And that makes a difference. There was no direction to the shadows which fell from 5 AM till noon, no depth to the dull glow of the lamp in my room. By afternoon no rain is falling—yet everything has already been washed away. Tomorrow, I suppose, one might be able to begin rebuilding on the waste of the weather. But not now. Now there is time only for one more cup of tea—before great swarms of storm-chasing gnats close in to pick clean what remains of my day.

PATERNITY

13 March, 2000—Petulu, Bali—

He was trying to describe to me how he'd fainted in the maternity ward—not during his wife's labor, but afterwards when he'd entered her room and seen the nurse stick a needle into her arm. The language barrier between us called for a touch of drama. He rose from his seat on the porch, pausing for a moment. Then, whistling an over-the-precipice-in-a-cartoon tune, he did a little dance of descent, slowly, like a leaf falling in spirals. When I laughed, he protested that it was only because he hadn't eaten anything all that day—that he'd been there, since dawn, near his wife's bedside. But *he* was laughing now as well. What a charming falling leaf of a father you will make, I thought—so strong, yet so sensitive to gravity.

LUGGAGE

14 March, 2000—Petulu, Bali—

I am beginning to feel the real weight of all the reading I've done here this year. Squinting at that very big stack of books which, like a magician, I'd pulled from my very small suitcase on arrival, I can almost convince myself that if I shift its ballast from one side of my room to the other, the floor will begin to tip like the deck of a ship in peril. I remind myself that this *is* what I'd come for, this quiet and serious month all alone on page after page of the high seas. Last night, Wayan arrived on the porch with a pink plastic bowlful of *bubur*, the boiled red rice and herb porridge prescribed by the locals for all forms of intestinal derangement. He was busy with his family at home, with his wife and his infant son, and so he stayed only long enough to pour me a single glass of water—an elegant parting gesture, one that touched me with its simplicity. Despite the mosquitoes, I sat out in the garden for awhile before bedtime, the moon-swept skin of my knees and bare feet trembling with shadows. My books, heavier now than ever with all my added marginalia, were already packed away in preparation for this morning's departure for the coast. And with nothing left to do or read, I tried to visualize the step upon which I was sitting—I tried to picture it a day, or maybe a year, after I'd left, after I'd trudged off, lugging my two tons of lettered luggage behind me. Unexpectedly then, Wayan returned, materializing soundlessly from out of the darkness in the garden. He'd come to retrieve the precious pink plastic bowl, the empty glass. Suddenly lightheaded, I watched as he dissolved back into shadow, bearing his own journey's all but weightless indispensables.

UNMANAGEABLE, INSECURE

16 March, 2000—Kuta, Bali—

The wind begins to howl and the rain begins to fall in torrents the moment the car leaves Petulu. The roads quickly become so impassable that my driver, the spoiled younger brother of a local village elder, is unable to pepper me with his usual ingratiating questions about what he fantasizes is my privileged life of high finance overseas. He is far too busy worrying about his precious automobile—that absurd specimen of social status in which I have been forced to accept a ride when the jalopy I customarily reserve in advance refuses to start this morning. Waxed and polished to pointless perfection, given the lakes of mud and debris through which we are forced to navigate on inundated roads, its chassis is slung so impractically low that every few minutes some devastating imprecision in the terrain results in an awful bump or scrape beneath us. In combination with the effort needed to maintain his vacantly arrogant smile, these abrasions almost bring tears to the poor fellow's eyes. I forgive myself in advance for my lack of sympathy and, instead, marvel at the way the sheets of water overwhelming the wipers distort the landscape drowning beyond the curved glass of the windshield.

The hotel itself is flooded. I have to wade through six inches of water in the garden to reach my bungalow. And I have to assure what passes for *'management'* that such conditions are not a problem—suppressing my smile of selfish satisfaction when informed that all other paying guests have fled. It doesn't rain continuously. There *are* breaks between violent squalls. It's during one such break that I dash down to the shore to see just what the storm is doing to the surf. The lull doesn't last long however, and I am soon huddled under the furiously dripping eaves of a *'security kiosk'* at one of the hotels perched up on the bluff overlooking the ocean—sharing my shelter with a rag-tag band of hawkers and vendors, itinerant masseurs, street smart children distributing leaflets or scalping yesterday's newspaper, purveyors of fine popsicles and perfumes, playboys and pickpockets, all the riff-raff who wander, without umbrella, these tourist byways. A further lull finds me headed for home, hurrying past a series of abandoned swimming pools overflowing with rainwater—one littered with ragged fronds torn from its luxurious perimeter of palms, another one the grave of a whole row of half-submerged chaise-lounges sent skidding across slick blue tiles by gale force winds.

A few days later, I return to find the kiosk has vanished completely—without even a footprint of demolition. The bluff upon which it stood, or squatted, was an artificial one, a wall of sand heaped up, without foundation, to provide a decorative border and bulwark for the newly constructed hotel behind it. After several stormy high tides, all that's left of it is a row of coconut palms—some toppled completely, some titling at precipitous angles, their protruding roots clutching at a few remaining humps of dissolving sand. The *guard* has apparently been dismissed, his kiosk dismantled. There is no trace of security here.

SPILLED MILK

19 March, 2000—Kuta, Bali—

They are a family on vacation, husband and wife, and three small children—three young girls in skin tight spandex shorts, their long blond hair already braided and beaded in local tourist style. Apart from a sandy blue speedo, Dad wears nothing but a thin scowl so habitual it could have passed for no expression at all. Despite the fact that the youngest of his daughters is climbing all over him, from lap to shoulders, he seems confident that such antic energy calls for no response. That is, until she spills her milk, really spills it—drenching the table, splattering the floor, and moistening major parts of her parents. Dad immediately lashes out to strike his daughter, restraining himself a split-second before impact. He shouts, he picks the girl up roughly by the strap of something, and re-positions her a few infinite paces from the rest of the family—while Mom, who's not uttered a word, spends the next five minutes dabbing at her milk-splashed sandal with a napkin solicited imperiously from a shyly appalled waitress. Those members of the kitchen staff who emerge to mop the milk from the floor at the feet of the family, they are the only ones who pay any attention to the unfortunate child whose facial expression has come to resemble that mask which promptly resettles upon the features of her father. When all other eyes are averted, a fresh glass of milk is slipped onto the table within reach of the outcast—but it remains a gift untouched, a kindness unacknowledged.

THE QUEEN OF SOMEWHERE ELSE

21 March, 2000—Kuta, Bali—

It's a long hot walk back from the beach on afternoons when it isn't raining, the paving stones of these congested alleyways savaged by periodic flooding and helter-skelter municipal upgrades. Largely sedentary for the past month in the mountains, parked on my porch with my tea and my books—by now I've developed several nasty blisters on my feet where wet sand meets sandal, and these further impede my progress through ninety-degree chaos. The gutters that run beneath the narrow concrete sidewalks are being dredged. At this stage in the process, they are no more than open troughs filled with muddy sewage-scented run-off. Slim, sunbaked adolescent slave laborers in torn clothes wade through the sludge, clutching picks and hoes and mallets and other medieval implements of quotidian torment. The normally bustling streetside shops have been forced to throw warped wooden gangplanks across filthy moats to provide access to anyone interested in buying yet another cheap hat, towel, sarong, or macramé bracelet.

Having long since abandoned their useless hawking, three young female shopkeepers have settled down silently alongside the fetid canal. On the inner bank, in the shade of the shop's makeshift awning—a sheet of stained blue plastic anchored by some rocks and a rope—one girl sits and knits, while another leans forward on her drawn-up knees, idly examining portions of her face in a broken bit of barely silvered glass about the size of the palm of her hand. Set apart, a third girl is crouched down on the far side of the gutter, nearer the road. Unsheltered from the heat of the sun, she squints into space, a numbed snarl nesting in the wrinkles around her narrow dark eyes. Together they form a mythic tableau of indifference—but it isn't until the following day when I return to find all three of them knitting, that it occurs to me to christen them the three Fates. At first, I assume that the third girl has finally deigned to join her two sisters in the shade. But passing by, I soon see my error—the girl on the far side, in the sun, is still there. The third girl now knitting is an entirely new addition to the pantheon. As for the pariah, she is still crouched and sweating, still squinting and snarling, her bearing as royal as ever.

GRAY ODYSSEY

26 March, 2000—Kuta, Bali—

I wait until dark before heading back to my room. It is almost seven o'clock, and the date had been for five. I am confident that by now, after sunset, I'll be able to slip unnoticed from the shoreline into the narrow street that leads straight to my bungalow. I even choose a path across the sand and a gateway through the low stone wall that I've never used before—just to be safe, just to stay solitary. And, of course I run smack into him. He's been waiting there for the whole two hours, scouring the beach impatiently for some sign of his good gay fortune. Naturally, he is a bit steamed, but two 5,000-rupiah notes (ostensibly for a 'taxi' back home) help to take the harsher edges off rejection. Not wishing to damage his self-image any further, I make a point of mentioning how handsome he looks—groomed as he is for action—in his tight jeans and brand-new plastic sandals, in his spotless white t-shirt with the decal of the Playboy Bunny plastered over his heart.

As I get older, I feel there is almost an obligation to desire youth and innocence, and yet I can't quite muster more than passive bemusement. He, however, really *had* refused to take no for an answer. He'd accosted me in both directions, on the way out and then on the way home—the first time tugging coyly at the hair on my shoulders, the second time going so far as to tweak one of my nipples. "*Tinggi,*" he'd tittered, "*tall.*" And then he'd tried, gently, to guide my hand to the small brown aureoles almost imperceptible on his own smooth chest. In the hot sun his brown eyes were bright as pennies. My own felt bloodshot from swimming for hours in salt water. I'd told myself that I'd make the date with him only to get free, and so I lied—promising to meet him the next day on my way home from the beach, at precisely 5 pm.

That next day, at half *past* five, I deliberately stop in an unlicensed snack shack nestled in the dunes and enjoy an illicit lukewarm ginger-ale. The wrinkled old woman tending the iceless cooler is glad for the company, as well as the handful of coins, and we manage to chat for a while in rudimentary *Bahasa Indonesia* without saying much of anything at all. After that I take my long slow stroll into the sunset. As gray deepens to the black that is to win the duel with orange, I find myself standing ankle-deep in the water, watching a back-lit gaggle of boyish Japanese surfers bobbing about on their boards in the waves, playful as dolphins. How marvelous, I think, to be so young and so far from home, so free to float past all restraint—even with distant thunder threatening rain and darkness falling fast. Beyond them the world is on fire. Beyond them passes the shade of a single fishing trawler, antique in form—its carved prow, silhouetted by flame, rocked by the rhythm of the waves like the head of a somnolent dragon—Odysseus, still lost.

2001

IT'S SO QUIET YOU CAN HEAR
THE ANTS TALKING

*Each day seems full of itself, and yet it is only
a few colored beans and some straw lying on a dirt floor
in a mote-filled shaft of light.*

John Ashbery

RETURNING TO THE ROAD

28 March, 2001—Petulu, Bali—

Perhaps it's because I overstayed my usual year at home in New York City, perhaps that's why I was so assailed by doubts when the time of embarkation finally arrived. I kept thinking—maybe I'm too old for this, too old to just interrupt the flow of life like this, to cross frontiers and gamble with domestic securities. Yet it's hardly a gamble at this point, is it? Over time, I've spent so many months here that there is as much of domestic ritual on one island as on the other. Although the scrawny cat, its shrunken teat troubled by a single white kitten, may not be always the same one—still its presence here in pre-dawn darkness is a given. As is my cup of hot tea. And my plate of cold fried rice, purchased in town on my way from the airport yesterday afternoon. I've already made out my shopping list—peanuts, crackers, bananas, mangosteens, a thermos, shampoo, canned tuna, drinking water, no surprises. I've already doused myself with insect repellent. The clouds above aspire to burnt lemon, those below disperse toward pale ash—while from the tear between them emerges a limitless blue embroidered with awakened birds. Green enters the garden only a split second before the dull roar of traffic returns to worry the road.

PSYCHOPOMPUSS MINIMUS

31 March, 2001—Petulu, Bali—

The white kitten, always the same white kitten, but different—
this time frolicking on the dark stone steps leading up to the
Pura Dalem on the outskirts of the village, lingering playfully
at the threshold of the local *Temple of Death*. The steps are
daunting—monstrous blocks of mossy concrete that dwarf the
young, be they feline or human. Negotiating them becomes a
seemingly endless round of advance and retreat, crowned at last
by an unexpected tumble into and then out of difficulty, toward
victorious confusion. Suddenly I feel I am in the presence of
divinity, convinced—though I am not close enough to verify
the fact—that four winged white sandals grace the four white
paws of *The Kitten Hermes*. Together we head for home, one
pretending to lead, one pretending to follow.

SIVA'S NEW HOUSE

1 April, 2001—Petulu, Bali—

There is a new bungalow on the property, a traditional Timorese dwelling, shipped here in pieces and then reassembled in the garden several months ago—all this at great cost to the new eager owners of this persistently sleepy little hotel. Already the paving stones beneath it are covered with a pale veil of sawdust, as the wood mites deep within its beams and floorboards set to work devouring it. Back in New York City I have learned that a long cold winter or a few moments in a microwave will deal with such voracious stowaways. Neither of these is an option here in the jungle, and so the only other course of action is to continually feed their appetites: to build constantly, to replace. Even tin and cinderblock, even plastics have their fierce adversaries in this climate. Without due diligence, the entire island could be stripped clean of the man-made in a matter of decades—everything not consumed from within, overgrown from without. The whole relentlessly creative drive of the island seems but a balancing mechanism, a tug-of-war between art and death, between construction and destruction—with lots of dancing in between.

BLUE

2 April, 2001—Batubulan, Bali—

It's the wrong time of day to be driving home on a motorbike. The roads are congested with belching flatbed trucks crawling beneath their heavy loads, mostly timber and massive blocks of limestone—and I am learning the hard way that these are the designated hours to which the trafficking of such cargo is restricted. Yet there are other lighter loads as well. Traveling directly in front of me for about twenty minutes of relentless stop-and-go is an open pick-up piled high with freshly picked hydrangea blossoms, its bright warm alp of blue violet dominating the landscape ahead. It begins to rain, and the driver of the pick-up pulls over and hurries, barefoot and shirtless, from the cab of his truck to toss a blue plastic tarp over his load of flowers, to protect them—not so much from the rain, as from the rapidly rising wind which is gusting now and sending the blue panicles bouncing and rolling down the highway between vehicles. With traffic at a standstill once again, I watch the truck struggling to re-enter the queue, this time behind me—revealing, as its blue mountain moves at last, a young boy beyond it, a serious young boy trying to cross the road in the driving rain, the light blue of his school uniform soaked and deepened at sleeves and ankles despite the broad blue umbrella he grips with such determination.

THE POSITION OF MY PILLOW

9 April, 2001—Petulu, Bali—

My pillow must have been gray at 5AM this morning when I left it lying unnoticed on the edge of my rumpled bed. Everything else was gray—the bed itself, the porch tiles, the palms in the garden, even the tea I poured was gray, even the chipped cup that I poured my gray tea into. Yet returning to the bedroom an hour after sunrise, I spy a patch of brilliant yellow light hollowed out near one corner of my abandoned pillow. I'm convinced, absolutely, that nothing but my own head could have left it there. What dreams I must have had last night—to leave such a glowing impression on sleep! I ease myself into bed, careful not to disturb the position of my pillow, lowering my head gently back into that pocket of light. It's a perfect fit, and I feel its warmth, but the magic is already gone.

SIMPLE TABLE

10 April, 2001—Petulu, Bali—

A simple table, impervious to weather, round and low, four black iron legs topped with a slab of marble. And there's nothing on it, there never is, it sits out in the loneliest part of the garden and serves no purpose. I can't imagine why it's been placed there at all—other than to resist all adjectives. Then, this morning, there are petals on the table, three unexpected white petals which have drifted from a nearby branch. I may brush them off as I walk by, or the wind may do it—. But by tomorrow they will be gone.

THE ROOST

12 April, 2001—Petulu, Bali—

Waiting for a friend on his front porch, left alone with his wife and his sister and half-a-dozen other young girls busy mesmerizing identical wooden statues with identical sheets of sandpaper, I find that being at a loss for words here need not prove a source of discomfort. I settle into the rhythmic rasp and hiss that wears wood smooth. I trace occasional figures in the sawdust coating cool white porch tiles. A boy comes running toward the house clutching three bottles of sweetened tea. In his haste, he has lost one of his sandals. All the girls laugh and hoot, pointing to it on the path behind him. Sprawled out on the floor, they all stop working, they straighten up and cross their legs as, with exaggerated formality and a plastic straw, I am served one bottle of warm tea on a cracked glass guest tray. More laughter. And then legs are extended again, ankles crossed, toes splayed, and the sound of sanding once more rules the roost. The boy has parked himself across from me. As I bend down to sip from my straw, he does the same, and our eyes lock—with the shy, silent mirth of men.

FULL

There is no wall
       to it all.
Up, goes the widening ball
       till I fall.
              —Ronald Johnson

17 April, 2001—Petulu, Bali—

All hollows have been stuffed full. There's nothing quite like ceaseless activity to lend the world the lie of solidity—filling in all dip and curve until even the heart has heft, as if it were an apple sitting on a four-legged table, rather than a balloon tugging against its single string. How did it happen: all these tasks lined up end to end like urgent knots in a rope thrown over a chasm? Exhilarating, these feats of engineering—yet I can't help feeling that I have betrayed emptiness somehow, that I have somehow literalized time and so lost my intimacy with its depths. I manage to steal away only one or two hours each day, and these I lay beside me in the sun. Through the single half-opened eye that we share, drowsy with sweat stain and heat shimmer, time and I have been watching the same plume of bamboo each afternoon, watching it bow and sway in bare blue noon wind like the neck of a drunken giraffe searching for lost ground far below it.

I'll be finished with my packing by dusk—boxes filled, sealed, stacked, ready for pick-up first thing in the morning. That'll leave me less than 48 hours before departure, before take-off and landing. At this rate of acceleration I'll be dead in six weeks
balloon popped
string snipped
apple full
of worms.

SWEET HANGOVER

18 April, 2001—Petulu, Bali—

A little farewell party last night, a little kebab dinner for shy friends and mystified neighbors. Everyone smiled broadly and denied that the beef was burnt leather, though no one even pretended to eat more than a bite of it. Steamed white rice, the one thing my western currency hadn't paid for, was the only dish in demand. No one seemed to notice the little fortresses of moist cake that Wayan's son deposited at irregular intervals as he wandered on all fours across the floor tiles. Each time I got up to go to the kitchen or outside to fan the flames of the kebab inferno, I felt another one squished beneath my bare feet. Though no alcohol was served, this morning I am sitting on my own porch as if tending a hangover—picking sticky splats of coconut and little pancakes of pink and green rice flour from between my toes.

TWO LAST BIRDCALLS

19 April, 2001—Petulu, Bali—

I was awakened from my afternoon nap by the scream, outside my southern window, of a damsel in distress—one bound to a railroad track directly in the path of an oncoming locomotive. But instead of a damsel she was a bird, and instead of a railroad track she was fastened to a pinwheel, and the pinwheel was turning underwater, and the water was boiling. She's gone now, dead or rescued. Now it's just the usual wind in the palms, an occasional wasp's buzz, some monotone chirrups and twitters, and the sigh of my own sweat as it dries on the skin of my ears. Passing by my porch, the gardener makes his customary detour to gather up my breakfast dishes—one last time, for I am leaving in a few hours. I wait eagerly for that final birdcall, for the sound of the fork that invariably slips from the plate halfway to the kitchen, ringing once as it strikes against the stones of the path at his feet. I am not disappointed.

DISTANT FIGURE

24 April, 2001—Kuta, Bali—

He's left his sons ashore countless times—cresting the beachfront breakers in his outrigger, then paddling out to the fringe of surf that marks the shallows of the distant reef. Yet for me it is happening for the first time. At the water's edge the youngest of his boys are naked and splashing, trawling tide pools with a rag of a net, chasing shadows of shrimp. A little further out, two older boys are swimming with a dog. Another has abandoned his bicycle in the sand and is crouched at the end of the jetty on a pile of slippery stones. There is no wind, yet I can feel it in his hair. What *he* sees is a father gathering shellfish, racing the incoming tide. But what *I* see is a father walking on the surface of distant waters, leaning like a blind man on the long tilting pole he leads with—his empty boat behind him, anchored on the swell.

I find myself looking down at my feet as I turn to leave. They seem to be planted firmly on this stretch of sand littered with discarded shoreside offerings to the gods—a colorful confetti of torn petals and saffron rice kaleidoscoped anew by each receding wave. I feel suddenly as if it is I that am being watched. I raise my head in the direction of the walker on the water, but a shout from ashore distracts me. A sun-bronzed boy in his underwear, soaked to the skin, has kicked his soccer ball in my direction. He dares me with youthful bravado, then just shrugs as I decline to return his serve, and goes on playing exuberant solitaire. Should he glance up now and again, he will see my figure grow smaller and smaller in the distance. By the time father has rejoined all of his many sons on shore, I will have vanished completely.

ABOUT THE AUTHOR

R. NEMO HILL is the author of a novel, *Pilgrim's Feather* (Quantuck Lane, 2002) a poem based on a story by H. P. Lovecraft, *The Strange Music Of Erich Zann* (Hippocampus, 2004), and three books of poetry from Dos Madres Press, *When Men Bow Down* (2012), *In No Man's Ear* (2016) and *Magellan's Reveries* (2018) He is editor and publisher of EXOT Books, at exotbooks.com.

He lives like an aging landlocked sailor in the Catskill Mountains, with his husband Julio. They just might 'set sail' once more, together this time—no one knows what the future holds. But at the present moment, this volume holds only a past that has become as vast as the future once was.

OTHER BOOKS BY R. NEMO HILL
PUBLISHED BY DOS MADRES PRESS

WHEN MEN BOW DOWN (2012)
IN NO MAN'S EAR (2016)
MAGELLAN'S REVERIES (2019)

HE IS ALSO INCLUDED IN:
REALMS OF THE MOTHERS:
THE FIRST DECADE OF DOS MADRES PRESS - 2016

FOR THE FULL DOS MADRES PRESS CATALOG:
www.dosmadres.com